'In this empirically rich account, Alice Gerlach offers extensive evidence of the ways in which immigration detention erodes women's sense of dignity and self-worth during their confinement and long afterwards. As the use of detention continues to contract in the UK in response to the Covid-19 pandemic, this book spurs us on to roll back this practice altogether. The women's accounts, which have been sensitively gathered, illuminate the deep pain this practice causes and its long-term effects.'

– *Professor Mary Bosworth, Centre for Criminology, University of Oxford*

'Within the increasing academic literature on border criminology, there remains limited empirical research on immigration detention, and less still on women's experiences. Alice Gerlach's book expertly addresses this substantial gap in knowledge. Drawing on the concept of dignity, this valuable addition to the literature unfolds women's experiences of the pains of immigration detention, and the challenges of social reintegration following deportation.'

– *Dr Hindpal Singh Bhui, HM Inspectorate of Prisons Inspector, and Visiting Professor, Centre for Criminology, University of Oxford*

DIGNITY, WOMEN, AND IMMIGRATION DETENTION

This book explores the experience of immigration enforcement for women who have been detained in immigration detention in the UK. Drawing upon in-depth interviews with women who have been in immigration detention centres, *Dignity, Women, and Immigration Detention* demonstrates how immigration detention violates women's sense of dignity and in doing so, causes women to suffer pains that are incongruent with the administrative purpose of immigration removal centres.

The women interviewed were either detained in an immigration removal centre, had spent time in this centre before being released into the UK community, or had been removed to Jamaica following time in immigration detention. This book argues that the current system used by the UK government is unfit for purpose and damaging to many of those who are ensnared within it. In examining dignity violation, lack of autonomy, and diminishment, the book also considers possible alternatives to the current practice of incarceration and what can be done to alleviate the harms that are currently inflicted on women during the process of immigration enforcement in the UK.

An accessible and compelling read, this book will appeal to students, scholars, and practitioners in criminology, sociology, law, social policy, and all those interested in listening to the unheard voices of detained women.

Alice Gerlach is Senior Lecturer in Criminology at Oxford Brookes University, UK.

Routledge Studies in Criminal Justice, Borders and Citizenship

Globalizing forces have had a profound impact on the nature of contemporary criminal justice and law more generally. This is evident in the increasing salience of borders and mobility in the production of illegality and social exclusion. *Routledge Studies in Criminal Justice, Borders and Citizenship* showcases contemporary studies that connect criminological scholarship to migration studies and explore the intellectual resonances between the two. It provides an opportunity to reflect on the theoretical and methodological challenges posed by mass mobility and its control. By doing that, it charts an intellectual space and establishes a theoretical tradition within criminology to house scholars of immigration control, race, and citizenship including those who traditionally publish *either* in general criminological *or* in anthropological, sociological, refugee studies, human rights and other publications.

Edited by Mary Bosworth, University of Oxford, Katja Franko, University of Oslo and Sharon Pickering, Monash University

Re-thinking the Political Economy of Immigration Control
A Comparative Analysis
Lea Sitkin

Border Frictions
Gender, Generation and Technology on the Frontline
Karine Côté-Boucher

Policing Mobility Regimes
Frontex and the Production of the European Borderscape
Giuseppe Campesi

Gendered Labour, Everyday Security and Migration
An Examination of Domestic Work and Domestic Workers' Experiences in Singapore and Hong Kong
Shih Joo Tan

Dignity, Women, and Immigration Detention
Alice Gerlach

For more information about this series, please visit: https://www.routledge.com/criminology/series/CJBC

DIGNITY, WOMEN, AND IMMIGRATION DETENTION

Alice Gerlach

Routledge
Taylor & Francis Group
LONDON AND NEW YORK

Designed cover image: Klaus Vedfelt

First published 2023
by Routledge
4 Park Square, Milton Park, Abingdon, Oxon OX14 4RN

and by Routledge
605 Third Avenue, New York, NY 10158

Routledge is an imprint of the Taylor & Francis Group, an informa business

British Library Cataloguing-in-Publication Data
A catalogue record for this book is available from the British Library

Library of Congress Cataloging-in-Publication Data
Names: Gerlach, Alice, author.
Title: Dignity, women, and immigration detention/Alice Gerlach.
Description: Abingdon, Oxon; New York, NY: Routledge, 2023. | Includes bibliographical references and index. |
Identifiers: LCCN 2022042700 | ISBN 9780367422806 (hardback) | ISBN 9781032410814 (paperback) | ISBN 9780367823153 (ebook)
Subjects: LCSH: Great Britain–Emigration and immigration–Government policy. | Women–Great Britain–Social conditions. | Noncitizen detention centers–Great Britain. | Dignity–Great Britain. | Women–Jamaica–Social conditions.
Classification: LCC JV7633 .G48 2023 | DDC 362.83/98120941–dc23/eng/20221109
LC record available at https://lccn.loc.gov/2022042700

ISBN: 978-0-367-42280-6 (hbk)
ISBN: 978-1-032-41081-4 (pbk)
ISBN: 978-0-367-82315-3 (ebk)

DOI: 10.4324/9780367823153

Typeset in Bembo
by Deanta Global Publishing Services, Chennai, India

For Pop up the road. *Tapadh leat.*

CONTENTS

INTRODUCTION

I still remember my first visit to an immigration removal centre. It sticks in my mind as a critical juncture in my life, where I stumbled upon something so troubling that I could not ignore it, and it has since sent me on a completely different trajectory in life than I would have followed otherwise. I had recently started a new job working as a researcher for HM Inspectorate of Prisons (HMIP), where my main role was to travel throughout the United Kingdom (UK) to places of incarceration, mostly prisons, and help to inspect their performance based on human rights obligations and standards. My particular role as a researcher involved conducting questionnaire-based surveys with prisoners. It was, and remains, one of the most enjoyable working positions I have ever held.

In the three or so years I worked at HMIP, I travelled to upwards of 30 prisons across the UK, and from doing this had a pretty good sense of the general 'feel' of prisons, from an outsider's perspective. There are notable variations in standards of care between prisons across the country, but, on the whole, prisons in the UK all had a similar feel to them.[1] The prisoners I spoke to, for the most part, understood why they were in prison. They had committed a crime, been caught, and were now serving the time handed to them. Their sentence was justified and largely based on sentencing guidelines, statutes, and the discretion of a judge. Prisoners were typically accepting of this arrangement, though

DOI: 10.4324/9780367823153-1

in most cases would, naturally, prefer not to be in prison. At the end of each prison inspection, I returned to the office, analysed the data, and passed the results to inspection staff with a general sense of a job complete. Immigration detention was different. I remember the second morning of my first ever visit. As I stood at a train station in London, waiting for a train to take me to the outskirts of London where the removal centre was located, I felt an overwhelming sense of dread and disquiet at the thought of going back. There is something uneasy about immigration removal centres. The best way I can think to describe it is an underlying sense of distress. I did not sense this unease in any of the prisons I had visited, not even in those I would consider the worst ones.

The sense of disquiet I felt when in removal centres stayed with me as a nagging sense of discomfort long after inspections were finished. The sense of a job complete experienced after prison visits was never there, and I found myself regularly troubled by interactions I had with both staff and the people held within the centres. Despite multiple trips to different removal centres, this feeling never went away, and I found myself wanting to understand more about them and the people held there. The result of that drive to understand is this book, within which I try to explain what makes the centres so distinctly troubling.

What is an immigration removal centre?

Although states have had the power to deport or deny entry to foreign nationals for many years, the systematic practice of immigration detention is relatively new. In the UK,[2] the current system of immigration detention has its roots in the Harmondsworth Detention Unit which opened in 1970 (Bosworth, 2014). There are many different pathways that can lead someone into immigration detention. New entrants to the UK can be detained while their right to entry is decided and then to await removal if entry is refused. Longer-term residents of the UK can be apprehended for overstaying or violating the terms of their visa, others are held if it is believed they have obtained their visas by deception or because they have been in the UK without valid visa documentation. Former foreign national prisoners subject to a prison sentence of longer than 12 months can be detained following their sentence, including those who have previously been granted permanent leave to remain in the UK. Individuals from any of the pathways above can also be kept in detention while a claim for asylum is investigated (Silverman and Hajela, 2013).

The number of people held in detention has steadily increased since Harmondsworth first opened in 1970, reaching a peak of 32,447 men and women entering detention in 2015 (Home Office, 2021). The year 2015, coincidentally, is also when the research for this book was conducted. At this peak point, the detention estate had approximately 3,500 bed spaces, typically filled by between 2,000 and 3,000 individuals at any one time (Silverman and Hajela, 2013) with a high turnover of people entering then leaving detention. The figures show 33,226 people left detention throughout the 2015; 15,106 people were subsequently removed from the United Kingdom; 180 were granted leave to remain or enter the UK; 17,540 were released into the UK community on 'bail'; and 400 were classified as leaving for 'Other' reasons.[3]

Since 2015, the practice of detention has scaled down, reaching a low of 24,480 entering detention in the year ending 2019 with 1,367 people held at the time of counting in December of that year. In the year ending 2020, things had changed dramatically as a result of the global pandemic, declining to 14,773 people entering detention and 910 in detention at the time of counting in December of that year. However, the latest data release suggests that there were 1,033 people in detention in March 2021, which may indicate a return to business as usual. This data does not include people detained for immigration purposes in prisons, police holding cells, or in closed mental hospitals.

There is no limit to the time individuals can be kept in immigration detention, other than pregnant women and families.[4] However, court proceedings against the Home Office have held that detention is only lawful if an individual's removal from the UK is a realistic prospect within a 'reasonable' period of time (HMIP and ICIBI, 2012). While 'reasonable' is sufficiently vague a term to allow long spells of detention for some individuals, the benchmark described within the Guidance on Immigration Bail for Judges of the First-tier Tribunal (Immigration and Asylum Chamber) suggests, 'three months would be considered a substantial period of time and six months a long period. Imperative considerations of public safety may be necessary to justify detention in excess of six months' (Tribunals Judiciary, 2018: 2).

How long people are held in detention is difficult to calculate because people can be detained, released, then detained again over time. There was cumulative time in detention data available between 2010 and 2014, but this has since been discontinued. Data that is available suggests that in December 2015 there were 263 people who had been held in excess of six months, including 6 who had been held between two and three years, and 2 between three and four years. The remaining population had been held between three and six months (401) and less than three months (1,943) (Home Office, 2021). These statistics demonstrate that a considerable number of individuals are being detained for lengthy periods. These data also show that the number of lives impacted by detention is substantial. Not only are large numbers of people a year still passing through detention, even during a global pandemic, their families and friends are also affected, as their mothers, fathers, colleagues, and neighbours are removed from their lives for an indefinite period of time.

People are not taken into detention as an end in itself, but as a means towards the ultimate outcome of expulsion from the UK. There is therefore more to the story than the detention itself. People are removed from the country and must then build or rebuild their lives there, or people are released into the UK community. In 2015, the percentage of people released was around 50 per cent but grew to around 60 per cent in 2019.[5] To gain a full appreciation and understanding of immigration detention then, we must look to what happens to people after they are released or removed from their incarceration.

Release

The purpose of immigration detention is to hold people before their imminent removal from the UK. However, approximately 50 per cent of people who are incarcerated in immigration removal centres are released into the community (Home Office, 2016). Though this is a welcome outcome for most people, it presents an additional set of problems for those released. Men and women are often released quickly, with little warning. They cannot always control where they will be released and many suffer lasting mental health problems (Canning, 2017; Coffey, Kaplan, Sampson, and Tucci, 2010; Hacker, Chu, Arsenault, and Marlin, 2012; Robjant, Hassan, et al., 2009; Steel et al., 2011). Measures of mental health from research conducted in Australia found formerly detained people suffered from a range of mental health problems including depression, anxiety, and post-traumatic stress syndrome (PTSD). Participants also scored low on quality of life measures and reported debilitating issues with concentration and memory (Coffey et al., 2010). Other research, also conducted in Australia, compared the mental health outcomes of two different refugee groups. The first group had been granted temporary visas prior to arrival in Australia, entering the country without a period of detention. The second group were not able to obtain temporary visas prior to entry and as such had spent time in immigration detention. The results showed that people who had spent time in detention experienced increased psychological disturbance over time, while the control group who had not been detained experienced improvements in psychological disturbance over time. This is despite similar potentially traumatic experiences prior to their arrival to Australia (Steel et al., 2011).

Formerly detained people describe acute feelings of injustice and insecurity in the community. In the UK and Australia, release from detention does not necessarily, or typically, mean permanent residency status, and many people were released temporarily with the ongoing threat of another period of detention. Many individuals perceive this ongoing situation as further punishment (Coffey et al., 2010; Klein and Williams, 2012). Feelings of punishment are understandable, with formerly detained people from the UK sometimes required to wear ankle tags usually reserved for prisoners on parole. The tags often came with strict evening curfews. People felt shamed by the use of tagging, and coupled with the use of a voucher currency system required to buy essential items like food and clothing, the situation of this group was made obvious to other members of the community (Klein and Williams, 2012).

According to Bail for Immigration Detainees (BID), people released in the community felt marked by their detention and lived in fear of being detained again with many reporting haunting dreams of their time in removal centres (BID, 2009). Logistical difficulties made life difficult for many of the released population who were reliant on the Home Office for their welfare. As an example, one man was granted refugee status after 3.5 years in detention in the UK. At the time of interview, he had been waiting over six months in the community for his official papers from the Home Office. This delay had left him unable to work, despite being legally able to. He was dependent on asylum vouchers (BID, 2009). Others had similar difficulties finding the means to support themselves and their families, both in the UK and Australia (Canning, 2017; Coffey et al., 2010; Klein and Williams, 2012). Those in the UK struggled to survive on approximately £37 per week. They vented their frustration with this system, particularly in their lack of ability to save towards their future with any unused funds wiped from their cards at the end of the week. They were also restricted from working and so had no means to add to their weekly ration (Canning, 2017; Klein and Williams, 2012).

In her research with females seeking asylum living in Merseyside in the UK, Canning suggests the destitution faced by women while they await asylum decisions is structural violence (Canning, 2017). Others suggest the practice of restriction dehumanises people seeking asylum through social exclusion (Bloch and Schuster, 2005; Sales, 2002, 2007; Schuster and Solomos, 2004; Tyler, 2006, 2013). Jurado et al. argue further that the government of the UK have deliberately moulded the conditions of social exclusion in order to ensure the migration pathways of this population are reversible (Jurado et al., 2013). Through exclusion, people are unable to build the community networks that may help them to fight removal from the country (Canning, 2017).

People released into the community also reported a negative transformation to their sense of self as a result of their detention. Individuals presented this change as a general loss of agency and in a sense of having failed in their carer, protector, and provider family roles. Loss of agency was described as a loss of initiative or sense of ability to acquire new skills or sustain work or study. In addition, they reported feelings of demoralisation, helplessness, and powerlessness (Coffey et al., 2010): 'I don't feel like me, people they can't ask me why. They just look. I'm not fine, but what can I do? I'm not fine. It's really hard' (BID, 2009: 46). Some felt they no longer belonged in the UK; where before their sense of self was tied to the notion that the UK was their home, detention left them feeling unwanted (BID, 2009; Hasselberg, 2016; Turnbull, 2016).

Further, men and women in the community reported relationship difficulties and breakdowns after detention, making it difficult for them to integrate or reintegrate into the community (Griffiths, 2013; Hasselberg, 2016). Some isolated themselves from social situations to avoid the anxiety this caused (Coffey et al., 2010; Steel et al., 2011). In the words of one man: 'As a normal human being I don't have the courage to talk to people, normally. After four, five minutes my entire body will be shaking or shivery' (Coffey et al., 2010: 2075). In the UK, people were shown to be relocated to arbitrary locations, with no regard for the personal connections and ties that may have been formed before detention or used to help reintegrate back in to the community (Klein and Williams, 2012). Some people described relationship breakdowns as they were no longer able to relate to their partner after substantial time apart (Griffiths, 2013; Hasselberg, 2016). Others returned home to find their children traumatised by separation during their detention, and some were unable to be reunited with their children as they had been housed in accommodation that was only suitable for single adults (BID, 2013).

Removal

Removal from the UK is an irreversible journey for most people, who are unable to return legally for visa reasons or otherwise for financial reasons (Miller, 2012). Little is known about the situation of formerly detained people once they have been removed from the UK, with the notable exception of the work of Turnbull (2017). In her work, Turnbull offers a brief investigation into the lives of nine informants who had returned to their 'home' nations from detention. The stories of the seven men and two women in this study were diverse, some were detained and returned following a prison sentence, others for overstaying student visas or during an attempt to claim asylum in the UK. Yet, their experiences post-detention and removal include similar narratives relating to their time in removal centres in the UK. Immigration detention and deportation were not well understood in their home nations. Removal centres were perceived as punitive, and the people who had been detained within them seen as 'guilty' by association (Turnbull, 2017). As a result, the people removed often tried to hide their detention from their fellow countrymen to avoid the associated stigma. Their attempts to hide this incarceration restricted their ability to integrate fully, and openly, and they were unable to obtain the support they required. This led to isolation, and an inability to seek support to deal with distress of their removal (Turnbull, 2017).

Men and women are taken to immigration removal centres with little to no notice (Turnbull, 2016; see also: Hasselberg, 2016). They are unable to collect their personal belongings, and must rely on their family and friends, if they have them, to retrieve any possessions they wish to take to their country of return. In a practical sense, this stopped men and women from preparing what would help them to (re-)integrate on arrival. Sudden detention does not allow people time to sell possessions, withdraw funds from bank accounts, or collect items such as valuable electronics or certificates of achievement required for employment. In Turnbull's work, this inability to prepare is linked with feelings of indignity and injustice, where men and women feel they are being disproportionally punished (Turnbull, 2017). People felt humiliated by their return when they had nothing to show from their time in the UK, and the punitive nature of this practice stayed with men and women once they had been removed (Turnbull, 2017).

Psychological distress was a defining feature of the lives of some of the men and women in Turnbull's research. People struggled to cope with the financial, emotional, and social challenges faced on return. Beata[6] had sought asylum in the UK and had been removed when her case was dismissed as false. Beata was unable to seek help from her family due to the reasons she sought asylum in the first instance, and two years on from her deportation was suffering from severe depression. She also lost her employment due to her declining mental health (Turnbull, 2017). Beata's story is an example of how the mental and physical health problems illustrated in the detention literature are carried with people after their expulsion. Detention can be the cause of new vulnerabilities and exacerbate old mental and physical health problems, and these can have a bearing upon an individual's ability to cope with the additional stress caused by removal from the UK (Turnbull, 2017).

Detention aside, existing research also shows a myriad of negative outcomes for men and women deported from their host countries, regardless of their pathways to removal (Bloch and Schuster, 2005; Miller, 2012; Griffin, 2009; Dolan et al., 2009; Schuster and Majidi, 2013; Golash-Boza, 2015; Brotherton and Barrios, 2009). Many removed people do not have ready access to cash or assets (Griffin, 2009). Those removed to Jamaica, for example, were reliant on other family members for accommodation and money to survive (Golash-Boza, 2015). Those without family or who had been rejected by their family had migrated to urban centres, often living on the streets (Miller, 2012). Men in Afghanistan were often found to have paid substantial monies to third parties to assist their initial migration attempts, and so on return they were left with related debts they were unable to repay (Schuster and Majidi, 2013).

Many people are labelled as 'deportees' on return to their home nations. This label carried with it negative social associations in most of the countries the research has been conducted. Those removed from the United States to the Dominican Republic suffered from cultural estrangement and stigmatisation upon return (Brotherton and Barrios, 2009). Men returned to the Dominican Republic found formal employment difficult due to the perception that deported men were criminal and to be feared (Golash-Boza and Ceciliano Navarro, 2017). In Jamaica, this group felt similarly criminalised and stigmatised (Golash-Boza, 2015; Griffin, 2009; Miller, 2012; Turnbull, 2017). However, in Brazil,

Golash-Boza found people who are deported there from the United States to suffer from no stigma associated with their forced return to the country. Similarly, men returned to Guatemala were not assumed to be criminal unless they had tattoos (Golash-Boza, 2015). Though, if a man removed to Guatemala did have tattoos, they were likely to face severe criminalisation and stigma from the general public and harassment from the police. Men with tattoos were also mistaken for rival gang members and were at risk of violence as a result (Golash-Boza, 2015).

In countries where being returned did not necessarily equate to the label of 'criminal,' people still suffered from stigma after their return (Golash-Boza and Navarro, 2017; Majidi, 2017; Schuster and Majidi, 2013). Men in Afghanistan felt shamed by their failure to successfully migrate and support their families and were subjected to negative perceptions of 'contamination' by their communities (Schuster and Majidi, 2013). The gendered notion that males should be providing for families also caused difficulties for men who were not able to fulfil this role on their return (Golash-Boza, 2015; Turnbull, 2017). In Turnbull's work, the failure to fulfil the role of breadwinner took an emotional toll on participants, and some had suffered the breakdown of relationships as a result. As an example, Adel, who was removed to Morocco, was no longer considered a suitable son-in-law in the eyes of his fiancée's family, who called off the engagement. He considered himself 'marked' by his detention and removal and had been presumed incapable of performing the role of future provider (Turnbull, 2017).

Individuals were moved from their family, friends, and sometimes children. They were returned to cultures and societies with which they are no longer familiar and in some cases have never known, having been raised in the UK from a young age (BID, 2013; Bosworth, 2011a). This lack of familiarity had a profound effect on their sense of self. Research conducted by Brotherton and Barrios with American deportees in the Dominican Republic showed people who struggled to reconcile their American identities with their new situation, with all personal reference points related to their American self. However, they were unable to express their American identities, for fear of the negative labels applied to removed Dominican-Americans (Brotherton and Barrios, 2009). In Afghanistan, men and women are increasingly facing living in 'limbo' as they are unable to return to homes that have been eradicated by the war or are too unstable to return to safely. Instead, Majidi recalls men and women living near the border areas they are forcibly returned to, where they hope to make another attempt at migration (Majidi, 2017).

The literature described above relates to the practical, social, and psychological impact of removal on people. There have also been more extreme examples where removal has been physically dangerous. In a report from Medical Justice (Medical Justice, 2012), two formerly tortured individuals had been forcibly removed from detention in the UK only to be tortured again upon arrival in their home nations. These stories are only known because both people fled to the UK a second time. Both were also detained upon their return. In a recent report on removal escorts from the UK to Nigeria, HMIP inspectors witnessed a woman with severe mental health needs being removed. During the journey to and on arrival in Nigeria she was severely distressed. She removed her clothes and took all the medication she had been provided for removal, including anti-psychotic drugs. After a failed attempt by Nigerian officials to refuse her entry, she was taken to hospital. Information provided by the Home Office to HMIP states, she was discharged later the same day. It is not known what happened to her after this (HMIP, 2013a).

We cannot know how often such events occur since information relating to what happens to people once they have been removed from the UK is not routinely collected. These examples and those earlier in the text illustrate a severe lack of understanding of the consequences of detention and removal for men and women. Literature on removal shows that people are often left in situations even more difficult than that which caused them to migrate initially (Golash-Boza, 2015; Schuster and Majidi, 2013). In addition, people are often criminalised, stigmatised, and suffering from a sense of shame at their failure to succeed in their migration attempts (Golash-Boza, 2015; Majidi, 2017; Schuster and Majidi, 2013; Turnbull, 2017). This, coupled with the emotional distress of separation from families and friends in adopted nations made resettlement incredibly difficult for most (Golash-Boza and Navarro, 2017; Turnbull, 2017). As a result, some people were found to be biding their time before another attempt at migration (Brotherton and Barrios, 2009; Golash-Boza, 2015; Majidi, 2017; Schuster and Majidi, 2013).

Conducting research with women from detention

I spent one year conducting the fieldwork for this book. I interviewed participants in Britain's women's detention centre, Yarl's Wood, women who had been released into the UK community, and a group of women who had been removed to Jamaica. In total, 76 women participated in interviews. Although detention is the focal point of this project, immigration removal centres are transitional spaces and time spent in detention can continue to define the lives of individuals after they leave (Klein and Williams, 2012). I sought to understand not just the experiences of women during their time in Yarl's Wood but also the impact their confinement had after they had left. Typically, people in detention are removed[7] from the UK to their nation of birth, a third country,[8] or released to an address in the UK. A small number are sent/returned to prison, to the care of a mental health institution, or die.[9] In addition to those in detention, I interviewed women who had been released to the community and removed/deported to Jamaica.

I began my research in Yarl's Wood Immigration Removal Centre in Bedford, UK, where I spent four weeks conducting interviews and making observations. All interviews were conducted in the last three weeks of my visit, as my first week was spent awaiting full security clearance from the Home Office.[10] During these three weeks, I conducted interviews with 38 women. Most interviews were conducted one to one (18), though some involved two women at one time (8),[11] and some involved three or more people at once (11). One interview became more of a focus group ranging in size from one interviewee to eight women discussing the conditions of the centre.

The second site was more diffuse. I conducted interviews with women who had been released from immigration detention into the UK. For this portion of the project, I met formerly detained women in London (2), the Midlands (7), Scotland (1), and North West England (2). Twelve occurred in total, all of which took place between January and December 2015. To recruit participants, I emailed organisations, support groups, and individuals who worked with formerly detained people. I met most of the participants in cafes or restaurants near to where they lived. Not only did this choice of location make it easier for them to meet, but the familiar surroundings made them feel more comfortable. Women were unlikely to attend interviews far from home because they could not pay for their travel.

My third research site was the island of Jamaica. This choice was largely practical, after narrowing my choices to countries that predominantly speak English, and then to countries where it would be relatively safe and practical for me to conduct fieldwork alone. I was also given the email address of an organisation in Jamaica called the National Organisation of Deported Migrants (NODM)[12] by another academic contact who had met NODM at a conference many years ago. After a couple of emails, it was established that they were willing to facilitate my research in principle.

I visited Jamaica on two occasions to conduct fieldwork. On my first trip, I spent two weeks meeting members of NODM and other organisations who work with people removed to the island. During this visit, I negotiated with NODM to access their databases[13] which held names and phone numbers of women (and men) who had been returned to Jamaica from the UK. I also arranged to work with two research assistants, Vinette and Ashley.[14] After my first visit, I returned to the UK to prepare for a longer visit of two months which took place six weeks later. During my second visit to Jamaica, I lived in an apartment on the campus of the University of the West Indies in uptown Kingston. Most interviews were conducted in a cafeteria in downtown Kingston. The cafeteria was in a new development for Digicel, a telecommunications company in Jamaica, and was located within walking distance of the main bus hub in Kingston. It was air conditioned and large, but quiet enough to hear clearly.

Meetings with women were organised by my research assistants, and I asked that each of the assistants organise two interviews each, per week, while I was in Jamaica. Vinette and Ashley initially called women from NODM's lists and asked if they had spent time in immigration detention in the UK. If they had, and were initially willing to be involved, they were added to a list of potential participants. At the beginning of each week, Vinette and Ashley would work their way through the list and arrange meetings with four women for that week. They would then call the women the day before the meet-up to remind them, again on the morning of the interview, and then finally at the time they were due to find out how far they were away. In more cases than not they had to find them and walk them to the meeting place. It was not uncommon for women to cancel the day before or on the morning we were due to meet. When this happened, Vinette and Ashley went back to their original list and found a replacement. My interviews were all attended by either Vinette or Ashley, who would greet the participant and introduce me to them. I would then move to another table to conduct the interview while Vinette or Ashley waited for us to finish.

From the outset, women began to tell me of others they knew who had spent time in detention before being removed to Jamaica. If these women were also interested in participating in my research, I asked that their details be passed on to the research assistants and in this way the sample list snowballed to the total number of 26 women interviewed.

Ethical considerations

Women in detention were powerless in many ways, held indefinitely, and most were being removed to countries and lives they were not willing to return to. The women I interviewed in the UK community were still under the influence of the Home Office, unable to work and in some cases destitute or very close to destitution. In Jamaica, almost all the women I interviewed were socioeconomically disadvantaged and lived precarious lives. As such, it was imperative to ensure additional precautions were adhered to in order to ensure no harm would be caused as a result of their participation in the study.

Not only were the women in this study vulnerable, they typically fit into the category of 'doubly vulnerable persons' used by Moore and Miller (1999). This term is used when a person fits more than one category that would have them classified as vulnerable. Taking the definition of vulnerable from Silva's (1995) text on ethical guidelines for nursing research, those most susceptible to vulnerability are those suffering from status inequalities that result in reduced autonomy. This is echoed by Moore and Miller (1999), who define vulnerability by the ability, or lack of, for people to self-determine their lives. There are some groups that are more prone to these characteristics than others, and they typically include immigrants, ethnic minorities, those from low socioeconomic backgrounds, LGBTG (Lesbian, Gay, Bisexual, and Transgender), and women (Liamputtong, 2007). Using these definitions, it is clear that the women included in this book are some of the most vulnerable populations it is possible to study.

I always sought to do no harm. The stories of the women I interviewed were sometimes distressing for them to retell, and they often became upset while discussing their precarious lives in detention, the UK or Jamaica. There is little research available on the potential to re-traumatise research participants (Sikweyiya and Jewkes, 2012); however, I agree with Sikweyiya and Jewkes that the likely impact of harm that *could* occur is a good enough reason to try avoid doing so. Therefore, whenever a participant became upset, I always asked women if they wanted a break and reminded them they could stop the interview at any time. In addition, I provided women with details of support organisations they could contact if they felt low after I had left. This was provided in the information sheet and I gave this to each participant before any discussion began wherever possible. I used my personal judgement at times and occasionally avoided sensitive topics women wanted to speak about. I was conflicted at these times between acquiring detailed and thorough data for the project and avoiding a discussion that would upset the participant. I felt responsible for their welfare in much the same way as described by Duncombe and Jessop (2012) in their discussion of rapport building and ethics. Here Duncombe and Jessop describe their guilt when the boundaries of researcher and friend were blurred or misconstrued and participants share more than expected about their experiences.

I had one particularly poignant example of this in Yarl's Wood when a participant, Cassie, began to describe in detail the death of her husband and her fears if returned to her country. She told me how she had never spoken to anyone about the trauma before, but felt comfortable enough with me to do so. She then disclosed intention to harm herself if she received removal directions. In practice, there is an expectation that researchers should obtain the consent of the individual before breaking confidentiality in a case such as this (Ritchie and Lewis, 2003; Wiles et al., 2008; Wright et al., 2004), and I had asked Cassie if there was anyone in the centre I could speak to on her behalf to tell them how she was feeling. She was unwilling to speak with anyone from the centre. I was torn, as the interview was confidential and I felt that I would be betraying her confidence and adding to her already substantial mistrust of people. However, I had good reason to believe she would harm herself in the likely event she was issued removal directions and so I reported her intent to a senior Home Office official in the centre. As a result of my actions, a security note was placed on her file instructing that she should be placed on a self-harm prevention plan when issued removal directions. This situation could have been avoided if I had declared at the beginning of the interview that I would need to report to the removal centre if any intent to self-harm was declared by a participant and I did this in many cases. Unfortunately, I had not before Cassie's interview. Before I was able to start speaking, Cassie began to tell her story and I felt there was no appropriate time to stop the interview before her declaration.

Another ethical consideration pertinent to this study was the use of incentives. The use of incentive payments for participants is common in qualitative research, particularly in many psychological and medical research studies (Silverman, 2013). The use of incentives can, however, introduce ethical concerns to the project; specifically that payment may coerce participants to take part in research (Barbour, 2008; Silverman, 2013). Barbour is sceptical of the influence of incentives for participants in social science research, and she argues that there is little harm in offering a reward for taking part in this type of research, particularly when compared against the risks of medical experiments (Barbour, 2008). Bioethicist Solomon Benetar similarly warns against mistaking incentives as coercion, particularly in the context of research in developing countries (Benatar, 2002). Benatar declares modest remuneration for time and travel expenses appropriate for research participation. In line with their views I, too, offered the women who participated in this project incentive to participate. However, in recognition of concerns regarding coercion, particularly with vulnerable populations, I made it clear to participants before interviews began that they were free to stop the interview at any point and they would still receive their incentive.

I offered women in detention a £5 voucher for the centre shop, after discussions with centre staff that this was a reasonable value. While a small number admitted that they were interested in speaking to me for the voucher there were many who were unaware and pleasantly surprised when it was offered to them at interview. Women in Jamaica were offered JA$2500 (approximately GBP£14) as an incentive for participation. This included an allowance for travel to the meeting point. This number was taken on advice from NODM, who made it very clear women would be unlikely to agree to an interview without incentives. Cash for travel was rolled into the full incentive in Jamaica as participants would not be able to procure receipts from bus or taxi journeys. JA$500 was calculated as the average price an individual would need to travel within Kingston to attend an interview. I offered women in the community £10 as an incentive to participate. I also paid their travel costs as needed. I had initially planned to provide the women with a gift voucher for Boots Pharmacy. However, after my first interview and informal discussions with NGOs, I replaced the voucher with £10 cash. This is because women in the community who are supported by the government survive on a voucher card system. These cards, and not having access to cash, was a particularly negative experience for women; therefore, I felt providing them with yet another card would be inappropriate.

Incentives were welcomed by most participants, though two declined to accept them. The first told me she was just happy to have given her story to someone. The second had a negative reaction to the offer of an incentive. I had written on my information sheet that I would be able to provide participants with a £10 cash incentive as a thank you for participating in the study, and when this information was read by this particular woman, she replied to my email with the following:

Thank you for your email.

> I have point about your offer in your letter as you wrote I can offer £10 cash for your participation
>
> Actually I'm not happy in this way!
>
> your research will be about dignity so you should know very well how to deal with this subject.
>
> This big offences to all women who you want to interview them!
>
> If you can delete this from your letter and your mind I will accept your interview if you can't
>
> I will not do interview. Sorry for that.
> Our pains is not for sale.

I was horrified that I had caused offence to this woman and that she felt I was trying to buy her story. I apologised for the offence caused and explained how her offence was exactly what I was trying to avoid by asking her about dignity and what it meant to her. She agreed to the interview after I sent her a revised information form without the incentive offer.

Reflexive considerations

The individuals in this project all identified as female. My choice to focus on women was, primarily, practical. There were eight immigration removal centres in the UK at the time of this study, but only one is designated to predominantly hold women.[15] Using Yarl's Wood as the site for immigration detention, I was able to visit one removal centre in the UK, but still concluded that my research findings were largely relevant to the female cohort of those in other immigration removal centres. This decision also left me with enough time to travel overseas and to interview women who remained in the UK after release.

My gender also allowed me to enter the rooms of women in detention, a space they described as one of few places in the removal centre where they felt comfortable speaking candidly. I would not feel comfortable alone in the rooms of men due to the inappropriateness this may suggest. In her book on immigration detention, Bosworth (2014) also writes that she and her female research assistants found securing an appropriate place to interview men in detention was a challenge due to fear of accusations of inappropriate behaviour (Bosworth, 2014: p.83). I also conducted my interviews alone with women who had been released in the UK. I often travelled to areas far from home. In these instances, I felt more comfortable that I was meeting a woman. As Jamieson (2000) mentioned in her discussion of conducting lone fieldwork, research with unfamiliar men and in unfamiliar surroundings has real and imagined risks that impact research.

Feminist researchers have long argued that the relationship between female interviewers and female participants can result in more fruitful data than male/female combinations (see, for example, Finch, 1984; Oakley, 1981). In the course of my research, my identity facilitated access to women, and for women to speak with me about vulnerabilities such as domestic violence and trafficking. However, I feel that it was the intersectional relationship between my gender and other factors such as perceived approachability and appearance and that not every female would have received the same welcome as I had.

My identity as a student and accompanying 'youthful' appearance were the most common factors women admitted as their reasons for agreeing to participate in my project. In Yarl's Wood, I found myself building the rapport of women much quicker and with an intensity that I did not anticipate. I expected to be treated as an intruder. For example, Bosworth (2014) sometimes found herself on the receiving end of hostility or mistrust from those women in immigration detention. As a student, I had been worried that people would not wish to waste their time talking to me. However, this was not the case. A number told me they were happy to have an interview as it would be helping someone with their studies. Many disclosed their dream of going back to school and earning a good education, and more than one said they wanted to meet me because attending Oxford University was a dream they had since they were children. It appeared that my identity as 'just a student' and my youthful appearance appeared to make women more open towards me. I sometimes felt I was being mothered, referred to as 'dear' or 'darling,' with women telling me how they had children at university, or who were similar in age to that which they perceived me to be.[16] Others, similar in age or younger, treated me as a co-conspirator, trying to 'help' me by giving advice on where I should conduct interviews or where I would best observe 'what really goes on.' One such participant introduced me to other women with the caveat 'it's ok, she isn't scary she's just a student you can talk to her.' As with those in Yarl's Wood, a number of Jamaican participants told me they had only agreed to be interviewed because I was a student, and that they want to help out someone getting an education. One woman expressed that she has had numerous requests for interviews in the past but had refused them all because she did not think she should help anyone make a profit from detention or help organisations that have never been of any help to her.

While my identity as a youthful student helped women trust me, other factors such as my identity as a white researcher were less effectual. The paper references earlier from Oakley (1981) and Finch (1984) suggest women interviewing women would extract more intimate data than if a man was conducting the same research. However, in this research they fail to address the differences between white, female researchers and ethnic minority research participants (Edwards, 1990; Horn, 1995). Alongside more recent papers on reflexivity in research (Belur, 2013; Edwards, 1990; Kamenou, 2007; Shinozaki, 2012) to ignore the possible impact of a white woman interviewing women of colour would be imprudent. Edwards (1990) is particularly critical of Finch and Oakley, when discussing in her paper the difficulties she had recruiting Black women to her study. She found some women were angered by the intrusion of a letter to their homes and complained to the gatekeepers who had given their private details to a white middle class woman. These difficulties were also experienced by Cannon et al. (1988) in their research into race and class bias in interviews. Issues of trust evident in the research of both Edwards and Cannon et al. were reflected in my own research. I found I had to go to great lengths to assure women of their anonymity and the confidentiality of the interviews. In Jamaica, my research assistants had to vouch for my credentials as an outsider, and it was clear that most women would not have attended interviews conducted by a white researcher without this endorsement.

My research assistants also had to vouch for me due to my nationality. I am a naturalised British citizen, born in Australia. However, I appear British to most people from outside Britain and I was perceived as such by most participants. When I interacted with the women's group in Birmingham, I was evidently an outsider, and this made me nervous. I had to go to some effort to illustrate to the women there that I was someone they could trust. It was only after offering homemade cake, describing my background, including my own immigration history and details of my marital status, that women were open to my presence at the group.

My immigration status as a naturalised British citizen drew interest from the women's group, who were curious how I had regulated my stay. At the same time, I was conscious that some women were frustrated by how easily I had become a permanent resident. In Jamaica, I was considered above all as a British citizen. My citizenship made me feel uncomfortable throughout the entire fieldwork process as I had a status that many of the women I interviewed wanted desperately. At the time of the research, I had spent approximately seven years in the United Kingdom, which was less than many of the women I had interviewed.

In Jamaica, I was also presumed to be wealthy as a British citizen. On advice from NODM, I asked my research assistants to explain to everyone that although I was from the UK, I was not in any way associated with the government and particularly the Home Office and would not be able to provide any assistance to the women. This strategy was largely effective in management of expectations; however, I was still asked by some women if I could help them to find information regarding their status and or help to find work. Cleona, who I interviewed in Jamaica, asked for help during her interview, after describing how she was struggling to get by:

> Me never have nobody to give me nothing, Miss Alice, nobody. But you know sometime you can mistake, you have to brush off and start back over. Miss Alice can you help me now, me want a nice little stove and a mattress, me eat and want, can you help me so I can buy it or they can help me buy it and …

Where the quote trails off I had interrupted Cleona and explained again my role and how I was unable to provide assistance. This intermission felt uncomfortable at the time, but I judged it was less hurtful to break the dialogue at this point than allow Cleona to continue to describe how the help I was unable to provide would aid her.

Although I was unable to provide financial or other practical assistance to women in the study, other than the small incentive payments for their time, their feedback after interviews was surprisingly positive. After the tape recorder had been turned off many told me they felt better for having spoken to me, that a weight was lifted of their shoulders. A fieldnote from the community reads: 'P. was happier at the end of the interview I think. She thanked me for my time and told me it felt like therapy for her.' In another interview, this time in Jamaica, the following quote was captured on my voice recorder of a conversation I had with a woman who was initially reluctant to participate. At the end of the interview, she asked how I was getting on with the research:

J: How's it been going so far?
A: It's been going really well, people seem open to talking to me.

> J: Yeah! I feel comfortable! Yeah! Cause I think it's a person, I never talk about it, never ever Alice, never ever talk about it. But I feel good now, cause it's like I get a burden off my shoulders. I tell you, I feel good! And I thank you for your interview, because I feel good!

These kinds of interactions made me feel that at least I was able to help women in some way. The nature of power in the relationship between myself and participants was imbalanced in my favour, and it was important to me that the emotive and difficult testimonies provided in interviews benefitted the women in some way. My guilt at being unable to help recipients is common (Dickson-Swift et al., 2007; Finch, 1984; Lofland, 2006; Oakley, 1981). In research with participants where the power relationship is imbalanced, such as with disadvantaged populations, the urge to help participants with their immediate needs is hard to ignore (Cannon et al., 1988; Goodrum and Keys, 2007; Mitchell and Irvine, 2008). There are many women who shared emotive stories with me, which I have no doubt will remain in my mind for a long time to come. However, I am unlikely to ever learn what happened next to them. Policy changes that may come from said research are also unlikely to help the women who offered their time for the study. That some women felt better after discussing their experiences with me also helped to alleviate this guilt.

Most importantly, in this particular piece of work, I used the subjective nature of dignity to help me remain as objective as possible. I sought, above all, to understand. I defined dignity based on what the women interviewed for the project believed the concept meant to them. I used focus groups to help interpret the findings and to ensure my interpretations of the data were recognisable and reflective of the population who participated in interviews. The themes that are reported throughout the empirical chapters of this book, likewise, reflect the issues which were important to the women involved. I have taken great care to avoid labelling their words with anything other than the framework of dignity that was derived from their words. While on the surface this may perhaps be academically simplistic, in my attempts to respect the dignity of my participants, I feel this was the right thing to do, ethically. It is, nonetheless, impossible for a qualitative researcher to fully claim objectivity in their work (Letherby et al., 2014; Ratner, 2002), and I have presented the above discussion on access, ethics, and reflexivity in light of this claim. In so doing, I hope that readers of this project will be able to assess for themselves the possible sources of research subjectivity and interpret the following findings with these considerations in mind.

What is the focus of this book?

Being subject to immigration enforcement is distressing. This is especially the case for those who have experienced immigration detention. This group of people appear to suffer from reduced self-worth, self-esteem, and their lives both in and post-detention are hindered by health problems, including PTSD, depression, stress, anxiety, and an array of physical symptoms that are often related (Cohen, 2008; McLoughlin & Warin, 2008; Robjant, Robbins, and Senior, 2009; Steel et al., 2011; Steel and Silove, 2001). There is very little in the literature to explain why people who have been in detention suffer in this way (although, see the Bosworth 2016 review in Shaw, 2016).

In this book I turn to the concept of dignity to help explain the pains of detention. In deploying this term, like others (see, for example, Jacobson, 2009; Mann, 1998; Miller and Keys, 2001), I refer to the sense that a person is worthy of a level of respect owed to them due to their status as a human being. Specifically, I explore the source of offence to dignity that immigration detention poses, and also what dignity *means* to the individuals involved and what happens when this is undermined. Literature on immigration detention suggests that people held in immigration removal centres in the UK are subject to treatment that damages their sense of dignity. This effect occurs despite legal and human rights protections (Van Zyl Smit and Snacken, 2009). It is therefore of interest to examine this disjuncture between experience and policy. Therefore, in this book, I explore how the experiences of women who have spent time in immigration detention relate to dignity. This is an important and neglected area of research, with available literature on immigration detention and its outcomes (see, for example, Bosworth,

2008; 2011; 2012; Bosworth and Kellezi, 2012; Steel et al., 2011; Coffey et al., 2010; Klein and Williams, 2012; Robjant et al., 2009; Griffin, 2009; Brotherton and Barrios, 2009; Miller, 2012; Schuster and Majidi, 2013), combined with the findings of HMIP (2013) and the High Court (Royal Courts of Justice, 2011a, 2011b, 2012) also suggesting that the dignity of those in detention is not sufficiently respected. The definition of dignity I utilise is a subjective and contextual one, defined by the subjects of this study: women who have spent time in removal centres. I focus on the resettlement of people from detention because their release or removal from detention is a critical juncture in their lives, and one that we know very little about. What little we do know suggests that life post-incarceration is substantially influenced by experiences in detention.

In the first chapter of this book, I explore the existing frameworks for dignity, of which are the basis for human rights frameworks, and that of dignity as utilised by the Home Office and companies that run immigration removal centres. In Chapter 2, I turn to the empirical data from women held in immigration detention at the time of interview. I explore the facets of immigration removal centres which women identified as affecting their sense of dignity. The areas for discussion are focused around the ways in which women feel criminalised and vilified by their time in these institutions. The unjust nature of detention described by women will be another focal point, alongside the indifference they described in their dealings with the Home Office. In Chapter 3, I move to consider the lives of women 'released' into the UK community after their detention. The themes for this chapter surround the impact of immigration detention and women's ongoing dependence on the Home Office after release. The criminalisation of women is discussed, in relation to the ongoing damage this had for those in the study. The restriction of women's ability to direct their own lives post-detention is also be highlighted, as is the perceived indifference of the Home Office to their situation post-detention. In Chapter 4, a case study of women removed to Jamaica is presented. Women removed to Jamaica faced precarious lives. They were labelled, stigmatised, and shunned by society, and as a result, it was difficult for women to find employment and to support themselves and their children. Their sense of self-worth suffered under these conditions. Women who had been removed after substantial time in the UK, under immigration powers, found their lives made more difficult by immigration enforcement practices that led to the loss of their possessions before removal. Alternatively, those who had spent time in prison were helped to return with the means to hide their status as returned citizens, bringing into question the relative pains of administrative removal vs deportation after time in prison. In the final chapter, I offer an analysis of dignity taking into account all three sites of investigation. Using the descriptions of dignity offered to me by women in the study, I attempt to define dignity as it was experienced by women who had spent time in immigration detention. Three prominent descriptions that were frequent throughout are discussed: Dignity as an action, dignity as a possession, and dignity as a state of being. Then, finally, these are analysed alongside literature pertaining to healthcare and prisons, as alternative sites where dignity is, in theory, experienced by individuals under the care of alternate institutions, and which could perhaps be utilised as examples to learn from.

Notes

1 I should note that things were changing towards the end of my time at HMIP, where I started to see some of the impact of austerity measures and budget cuts leading to a more unsettled prisoner population.

2 Though I use the term 'UK' here, I recognise that most literature used to inform this book is based on research conducted in the three nations of Britain: England, Scotland, and Wales. The political climate and immigration experience of those held in Northern Ireland is notably different (Canning, 2017). Thus, while some of the findings and themes will be relevant to this country, care should be taken to fully understand these in the context of the different socio-political landscape under which individuals in this country are residing.

3 'Other' includes people who have been returned to prison, some released with no conditions, i.e., they are no longer subject to immigration control, people who have been sectioned under the Mental Health Act, and people who have either died in detention or absconded from detention.

4 The rules surrounding pregnant women in detention were updated with the 2016 Immigration Bill. Once a woman has been discovered to be pregnant in immigration detention, she must now be released within 72 hours. Likewise, families with children should not be held in immigration removal centres; however, they can be held in 'pre-departure accommodation,' also for 72 hours. However, in both cases, ministerial review can be sought for an extended stay of up to a week (McGuiness and Gower, 2017).

5 Data from 2020 to 2021 have not been included in this analysis as the numbers are too heavily impacted by the global pandemic to be considered comparable.

6 A pseudonym.

7 In this context, I am using 'removed' as a coverall term. Technically there are three different types of 'removal' from the UK. 1. Deportation, where individuals are removed based on this act being 'conducive to the public good' by the Secretary of State, or if they are removed following a criminal

court proceeding. 2. Administrative Removal, where the removal of an individual is enforced after they have been found to have no right to stay in the UK. 3. Voluntary Removal, where procedures for an enforced removal have been started, but the person has left the country before the removal has been enforced.

8 There are also individuals who will be removed to the first safe EU country they entered, following the Dublin III regulation.

9 The Prisons and Probation Ombudsman holds the records of 29 deaths in immigration removal centres since 2004; they can be found at http://www.ppo.gov.uk/.

10 More details on methods to gain security clearance are found below in 'Access.'

11 One double interview resulted in only one consented interview, with the other interviewee withdrawing consent later.

12 NODM is an NGO in Jamaica which acts as a signposting service for people removed to the island. The organisation is run by a group of removed persons with some financial assistance from the British High Commission in Jamaica.

13 I did not access the databases personally; this was done by the research assistants who were members of NODM.

14 At their request, the names of the research assistants are pseudonyms to protect their privacy.

15 There are women's units in other removal centres that predominantly hold men.

16 This was usually 5 or more years less than my 29 years at the time.

References

Barbour R (2008) *Introducing Qualitative Research: A Student's Guide to the Craft of Doing Qualitative Research*. London: SAGE Publications, Ltd.

Belur J (2013) Status, gender and geography: Power negotiations in police research. *Qualitative Research* 14(2): 184–200. https://doi.org/10.1177/1468794112468474.

Benatar SR (2002) Reflections and recommendations on research ethics in developing countries. *Social Science and Medicine* 54(7): 1131–1141. https://doi.org/10.1016/S0277-9536(01)00327-6.

BID (2009) Out of sight, out of mind: Experiences of immigration detention in the UK what is bail for immigration detainees? Available at: http://www.biduk.org/download.php?id=6.

BID (2013) *Fractured Childhoods: The Separation of Families by Immigration Detention*. London: Bail for Immigration Detainees.

Bloch A and Schuster L (2005) At the extremes of exclusion: Deportation, detention and dispersal. *Ethnic and Racial Studies* 28(3): 491–512. https://doi.org/10.1080/0141987042000337858.

Bosworth M (2008) Immigration detention. *Criminal Justice Matters* 71(1): 24–25. https://doi.org/10.1080/09627250801937611.

Bosworth M (2011) Deportation, detention and foreign-national prisoners in England and Wales. *Citizenship Studies* 15(5): 583–595. https://doi.org/10.1080/13621025.2011.583789.

Bosworth M (2012) Subjectivity and identity in detention: Punishment and society in a global age. *Theoretical Criminology* 16(2): 123–140. https://doi.org/10.1177/1362480612441116.

Bosworth M (2014) *Inside Immigration Detention.* Oxford: Oxford University Press.

Bosworth M and Kellezi B (2012) Quality of life in detention: Results for MQLD questionnaire data collected in IRC Yarl's Wood, IRC Tinsley House, and IRC Brook House, August 2010 - Hune 2011. (February).

Brotherton DC and Barrios L (2009) Displacement and stigma: The social-psychological crisis of the deportee. *Crime, Media, Culture* 5(1): 29–55. https://doi.org/10.1177/1741659008102061.

Canning V (2017) *Gendered Harm and Structural Violence in the British Asylum System*. Abingdon: Routledge. https://doi.org/10.4324/9781315720975.

Cannon LW, Higginbotham E and Leung MLA (1988) Race and class bias in qualitative research on women. *Gender and Society* 2(4): 449–462. https://doi.org/10.1177/089124388002004003.

Coffey GJ, Kaplan I, Sampson RC and Tucci MM (2010) The meaning and mental health consequences of long-term immigration detention for people seeking asylum. *Social Science and Medicine*. 70(12): 2070–2079. https://doi.org/10.1016/j.socscimed.2010.02.042.

Cohen J (2008) Safe in our hands?: A study of suicide and self-harm in asylum seekers. *Journal of Forensic and Legal Medicine* 15(4): 235–244. https://doi.org/10.1016/j.jflm.2007.11.001.

Dickson-Swift V, James EL, Kippen S and Liamputtong P (2007) Doing sensitive research: What challenges do qualitative researchers face? *Qualitative Research* 7(3): 327–353. https://doi.org/10.1177/1468794107078515.

Dolan C, Schuster L and Merefield M (2009) *The Impact of Deportation: Some Reflections on Current Practice*, Kampala: Refugee Law Project.

Duncombe J and Jessop J (2012). 'Doing rapport and the ethics or "faking friendship." In Miller T, Birch M, Mauthner M, and Jessop J (Eds.), *Ethics in Qualitative Research* (2nd ed.). London: SAGE Publications, Ltd., pp. 108–121.

Edwards R (1990) Connecting method and epistemology: A white woman interviewing black women. *Women's Studies International Forum* 13(5): 477–490. https://doi.org/10.1016/0277-5395(90)90100-C.

Finch J (1984) 'It's great to have someone to talk to': The ethics and politics of interviewing women. In: Bell C and Roberts H (eds.) *Social Researching: Politics, Problems, Practice*. London: Routledge & Kegan Paul, pp. 70–87.

Golash-Boza T (2015) *Deported: Immigration Policing, Disposable Labour, and Global Capitalism*. New York and London: New York University Press.

Golash-Boza T and Ceciliano Navarro Y (2017) 'My whole life is in the USA': Dominican deportees' experiences of isolation, precarity, and resilience. In:

Khosravi S (ed.) *After Deportation: Ethnographic Perspectives*. London: Palgrave Macmillan, pp. 149–168.

Goodrum S and Keys JL (2007) Reflections on two studies of emotionally sensitive topics: Bereavement from murder and abortion. *International Journal of Social Research Methodology* 10(4): 249–258. https://doi.org/10.1080/13645570701400976.

Griffin CE (2009) Deportation and reintegration in the Caribbean and Latin America: Addressing the development–security paradox. In: Mcdonald WF (ed.) *Immigration, Crime and Justice: 13 (Sociology of Crime Law and Deviance)*. Bingley: Emerald Group Publishing, pp. 279–296. https://doi.org/10.1108/S1521-6136(2009)0000013018.

Griffiths M (2013) Living with uncertainty: Indefinite immigration detention. *Journal of Legal Anthropology* 1(3): 263–286. https://doi.org/10.4059/jla.2013.2616.

Hacker K, Chu J, Arsenault L and Marlin RP (2012) Provider's perspectives on the impact of Immigration and Customs Enforcement (ICE) activity on immigrant health. *Journal of Health Care for the Poor and Underserved*. https://doi.org/10.1353/hpu.2012.0052.

Hasselberg I (2016) *Enduring Uncertainty: Deportation, Punishment and Everyday Life*. Oxford: Berghahn.

HM Inspectorate of Prisons and Independent Chief Inspector of Borders and Immigration (2012) *The Effectiveness and Impact of Immigration Detention Casework: A Joint Thematic Review by HM Inspectorate of Prisons and the Independent Chief Inspector of Borders and Immigration December 2012*. London: HMIP

HMIP (2013a) *Detainees under Escort: Inspection of Escort and Removals to Nigeria and Ghana*. (November). London: HMIP

Home Office (2016) *Detention Tables 24*. London: Home Office.

Home Office (2021) *Detention Summary Tables March 2021*. London: Home Office.

Horn R (1995) II. Reflexivity in placement: Women interviewing women. *Feminism and Psychology* 5(1): 94–98. https://doi.org/10.1177/0959353595051009.

Jacobson N (2009) A taxonomy of dignity: A grounded theory study. *BMC International Health and Human Rights* 9: 3. https://doi.org/10.1186/1472-698X-9-3.

Jamieson J (2000) Danger in fieldwork on crime. In: Lee-Treweek G and Linkogle S (eds.) *Danger in the Field: Risk and Ethics in Social Research*. London: Routledge, pp. 61–71.

Jurado E, Brochmann G and Dølvik J (2013) *Immigration, Work and Welfare: Towards an Integrated Approach*. London: Policy Network.

Kamenou N (2007) Methodological considerations in conducting research across gender, 'race', ethnicity and culture: A challenge to context specificity in diversity research methods. *The International Journal of*

Human Resource Management 18(11): 1995–2010. https://doi.org/10.1080/09585190701638234.

Klein A and Williams L (2012) Immigration detention in the community: Research on the experiences of migrants released from detention centres in the UK. *Population, Space and Place* 18(6): 741–753. https://doi.org/10.1002/psp.1725.

Letherby G, Scott J and Williams M (2014) Objectivity and subjectivity in practice. In: *Objectivity and Subjectivity in Social Research*, pp. 103–126. https://doi.org/10.4135/9781473913929.

Lofland J (2006) *Analyzing Social Settings: A Guide to Qualitative Observation and Analysis*. 4th ed. Belmont, CA: Wadsworth/Thomson Learning Publication.

Majidi N (2017) Deportees lost at 'home': Post-deportation outcomes in Afghanistan. In: Khosravi S (ed.) *After Deportation: Ethnographic Perspectives*. London: Palgrave Macmillan, pp. 127–148.

Mann J (1998) Dignity and health: The UDHR's revolutionary first article. *Health and Human Rights* 3(2): 31–38.

McGuiness T and Gower M (2017) *Immigration Detention in the UK: An Overview*. Briefing Paper Number 7294. London: House of Commons.

McLoughlin P and Warin M (2008) Corrosive places, inhuman spaces: Mental health in Australian immigration detention. *Health and Place* 14(2): 254–264. https://doi.org/10.1016/j.healthplace.2007.06.008.

Medical Justice (2012). *'The Second Torture': The Immigration Detention of Torture Survivors*. London: Medical Justice.

Miller A (2012) Deportation as a process of irreversible transformation. *Journal of Ethnic and Migration Studies* 38(May): 131–146. https://doi.org/10.1080/1369183X.2012.640024.

Miller AB and Keys CB (2001) Understanding dignity in the lives of homeless persons. *American Journal of Community Psychology* 29(2): 331–355.

Mitchell W and Irvine A (2008) I'm okay, you're okay?: Reflections on the well-being and ethical requirements of researchers and research participants in conducting qualitative fieldwork interviews. *International Journal of Qualitative Methods* 7(4): 31–44. Available at: https://ejournals.library.ualberta.ca/index.php/IJQM/article/view/4053.

Moore LW and Miller M (1999) Initiating research with doubly vulnerable populations. *Journal of Advanced Nursing* 30(5): 1034–1040. https://doi.org/10.1046/j.1365-2648.1999.01205.x.

Oakley A (1981) Interviewing women: A contradiction in terms. In: Roberts H (ed.) *Doing Feminist Research*. London and Boston, MA: Routledge and Kegan Paul, pp. 30–61.

Ratner C (2002) Subjectivity and objectivity in qualitative methodology. *Forum Qualitative Sozialforschung* 3(3). https://doi.org/10.4135/9781446222041.n18.

Ritchie J and Lewis J (2003) *Qualitative Research Practice: A Guide for Social Science Students and Researchers*. London: SAGE.

Robjant K, Hassan R and Katona C (2009) Mental health implications of detaining asylum seekers: Systematic review. *The British Journal of Psychiatry: The Journal of Mental Science* 194(4): 306–312. https://doi.org/10.1192/bjp.bp.108.053223.

Robjant K, Robbins I and Senior V (2009) Psychological distress amongst immigration detainees: A cross-sectional questionnaire study. *The British Journal of Clinical Psychology* 48(Pt 3): 275–286. https://doi.org/10.1348/014466508X397007.

Royal Courts of Justice (2011a) *BA v Secretary of State for the Home Department.* United Kingdom: High Court (England and Wales).

Royal Courts of Justice (2011b) *S v Secretary of State for the Home Department.* United Kingdom: High Court (England and Wales).

Royal Courts of Justice (2012) *HA Nigeria v Secretary of State for the Home Department.* United Kingdom: High Court (England and Wales), https://doi.org/10.5305/amerjintelaw.106.3.0616.

Sikweyiya Y and Jewkes R (2012) Perceptions and experiences of research participants on gender-based violence community based survey: Implications for ethical guidelines. *PLoS ONE* 7(4). https://doi.org/10.1371/journal.pone.0035495

Sales R (2002) The deserving and undeserving? Refugees, asylum seekers and welfare in Britain. *Critical Social Policy* 22(3): 456–478.

Sales R (2007) *Understanding Immigration and Refugee Policy: Contradictions and Continuities.* Bristol: Policy Press.

Schuster L and Majidi N (2013) What happens post-deportation? The experience of deported Afghans. *Migration Studies* 1(2): 221–240. https://doi.org/10.1093/migration/mns011.

Schuster L and Solomos J (2004) Race, immigration and asylum: New labour's agenda and its consequences. *Ethnicities* 4(2): 267–287. https://doi.org/10.1177/1468796804042606.

Shaw S (2016) *Review into the Welfare in Detention of Vulnerable Persons: A Report to the Home Office by Stephen Shaw.* London: HMSO, CM9186.

Shinozaki K (2012) Transnational dynamics in researching migrants: Self-reflexivity and boundary-drawing in fieldwork. *Ethnic and Racial Studies* 35(February 2015): 1810–1827. https://doi.org/10.1080/01419870.2012.659275.

Silva, M (1995) *Ethical Guidelines in the Conduct, Dissemination, and Implementation of Nursing Research.* Washington DC: American Nurses Publishing.

Silverman D (2013) *Doing Qualitative Research: A Practical Handbook.* 4th ed. London: SAGE Publications, Ltd.

Steel Z and Silove DM (2001) The mental health implications of detaining asylum seekers. *The Medical Journal of Australia* 175(11–12): 596–599.

Steel Z, Momartin S, Silove D, Coello M, Aroche J, Tay KW (2011) Two year psychosocial and mental health outcomes for refugees subjected to restrictive or supportive immigration policies. *Social Science and Medicine.* 72(7): 1149–1156. https://doi.org/10.1016/j.socscimed.2011.02.007.

Tribunals Judiciary (2018) Judge Clements, President of the First-tier Tribunal (Immigration and Asylum Chamber) Presidential Guidance Note No 1 of 2018: Guidance on Immigration Bail for Judges of the First-tier Tribunal (Immigration and Asylum Chamber). London: HMCTS.

Turnbull S (2016) 'Stuck in the middle': Waiting and uncertainty in immigration detention. *Time and Society* 25(1): 61–79. https://doi.org/10.1177/0961463X15604518.

Turnbull S (2017) Starting again: Life After deportation from the UK. In: Khosravi S (ed.) *After Deportation: Ethnographic Perspectives*. London: Palgrave Macmillan, pp. 37–62.

Tyler I (2006) 'Welcome to Britain': The cultural politics of asylum. *European Journal of Cultural Studies* 9(2): 185–202. https://doi.org/10.1177/1367549406063163.

Tyler I (2013) *Revolting Subjects: Social Abjection and Resistance in Neoliberal Britain*. London: Zed Books.

Van Zyl Smit D and Snacken S (2009) *Principles of European Prison Law and Policy: Penology and Human Rights*. Oxford: Oxford University Press.

Wiles R, Crow G, Heath S and Charles V (2008) The management of confidentiality and anonymity in social research. *International Journal of Social Research Methodology* 11(5): 417–428. https://doi.org/10.1080/13645570701622231.

Wright S, Waters R and Nicholls V (2004) Ethical considerations in service-user-led research: Strategies for living project. In: Smyth M and Williamson E (eds.) *Researchers and their 'Subjects': Ethics, Power, Knowledge, and Consent*. Bristol: Oxford University Press, pp. 19–34.

1

THE PROBLEM WITH DEFINING DIGNITY

The disquiet I first felt when visiting immigration removal centres has never really abated. In fact, I can no longer think of immigration detention without feeling a sense of discomfort. Like many others who do research within the field of border criminology, I feel that the further I explore the practices of immigration enforcement, the more strongly I feel that there is something fundamentally wrong about the system, both in the UK and internationally. What I offer in this chapter, and book, is an application of a new framework in border criminology, and that framework is the concept of dignity.

Dignity is a difficult concept to define, and, seemingly, an even more difficult concept to operationalise into practical behaviours and acts towards others. Yet, most of us know what it means to be treated with it. Dignity is brandished about regularly in popular culture. In the final Harry Potter book and film even the evil protagonist, Voldemort, invokes the concept with respect. Following his successful attack on Hogwarts, Voldemort commands his forces to retreat so that Potter and his allies can bury their dead 'with dignity' (Rowling, 2007; Yates, 2011). In the 2012 James Bond movie *Skyfall*, much of the film hinges on the fictional M's refusal to accept another agent's definition of dignity as retirement, instead preferring her own 'dignified' retirement planning: 'Oh, to hell with dignity. I'll leave when the job's done' (Mendes, 2012). Even the barman at one of my favourite pubs has a 'dignity' tattoo on his arm.[1]

What this common use of dignity alludes to is the idea that this sense of worth is important to people, however opaque its precise definition.

DOI: 10.4324/9780367823153-2

Markedly, the preoccupation with dignity in popular culture is when dignity is absent or threatened. To have dignity, it appears, is the norm and to have your sense of worth challenged is, therefore, a particularly offensive experience. Theorists of the concept arrive at similar conclusions, where violations to an individual's dignity have a greater impact on them than when their sense of self-worth is respected (Jacobson, 2010; Mann, 1998).

Defining dignity

Modern ideas of dignity are rooted in the work of philosopher Immanuel Kant (1996). Kant believed that dignity was an immutable human characteristic. To him, it was an inherent and inviolable part of being human, intimately related to our status as autonomous beings capable of moral rationality. Such characteristics, he asserted, morally constrain our interactions with one another in a way that is unmatched by any other being (Kant, 1996; Killmister, 2010; Kraynak and Tinder, 2003; Misztal, 2012; Rosen, 2012; Shell, 2003). This moral constraint, he argued, grants humans a higher worth and status than any other entity, because we have this characteristic we are deserving of a certain level of respect (Birnbacher, 1996; Kant, 1996; Meyer, 1989). In other words, we are morally aware that we, and others, deserve treatment of a particular, and higher, sort. Because we know this, we interpret acts which deviate from the respectful norm as exceptionally offensive. The term 'human dignity' is ascribed to Kant and those who discuss his original works on morality (Kraynak and Tinder, 2003; Shell, 2003; Sensen, 2009).

Human dignity has interested many scholars of philosophy, religion, and ethics, who are concerned with metaphysical discussions of the underlying assertions drawn by Kant (see, for example, Guerra, 2001; Johnson, 1971). Core arguments in these fields focus on such details as interpretation of the semantics used by Kant (Kolnai, 1976; Sensen, 2009) and how human beings have come to be endowed with dignity in the first instance (Dales, 1977; Guerra, 2001). Closer in relevance to the subject of this book, others accept the principles of human dignity, that it exists and all humans have it, and consider the moral responsibilities of humans in light of the concept (Dales, 1977; Johnson, 1971; Korsgaard, 1992).

Human dignity is particularly pertinent to the field of law and human rights, where it forms the basis of the principles set out in the Universal

Declaration of Human Rights (UDHR) (Donnelly, 1982; Dupre, 2009; Feldman, 1999, 2000; Habermas, 2010; Jacobson, 2007; Kraynak and Tinder, 2003; Misztal, 2012; Neal, 2014; Nordenfelt, 2004; Rosen, 2012; Rothhaar, 2010; Sensen, 2009b; Shell, 2003). Both the law and human rights-based deliberations on the concept have been important for the development of rights-based legal systems and world views. It is made abundantly clear through these instruments that human dignity is something that should be protected. Human dignity within the UDHR is the fundamental crux upon which the conceptual framework and arguments within this book are built. Therefore, I will take the time now to draw out how dignity in the UDHR is relevant to the United Kingdom and to immigration detention.

The UDHR was created after the atrocities committed during the Second World War. The preamble of the declaration makes reference to 'barbarous acts which have outraged the conscience of mankind' (United Nations, 1948), in which the drafters were most importantly referring to the mass humiliations and killings of the Holocaust (Margalit and Motzkin, 2006; Morsink, 2000). The treatment of the Jewish population at the hands of the Nazi Government of Germany was unprecedented, as despite a world history plagued by mass murders and mass humiliations, the world had never before seen the deliberate combination of the two that stripped people of their dignity in life and in death (Margalit and Motzkin, 2006). After the war, there was a collective outrage about these violations, and in reading the UDHR, it is clear to see that dignity is recognised to be of vital importance to individuals and societies (Morsink, 2000). The term appears first in the preamble:

> Whereas recognition of the inherent dignity and of the equal and inalienable rights of all members of the human family is the foundation of freedom, justice and peace in the world.

And again in Article 1:

> All human beings are born free and equal in dignity and rights. They are endowed with reason and conscience and should act towards one another in a spirit of brotherhood.
>
> *(United Nations, 1948)*

In the International Covenant on Economic, Social and Cultural Rights (ICESCR) and the International Covenant on Civil and Political Rights

(ICCPR), both of which were ratified by the UK in 1976, dignity is also posed as the basis from which all human rights treaties have been derived (McCrudden, 2008).

In order to protect the dignity of those, like the women I interviewed for this book, who are deprived of their liberty, the UK has subscribed to optional UN conventions. These conventions recognise that those whose liberty has been curtailed are particularly vulnerable to inhumane treatment and in need of extra protections (HMIP, 2014b). The British government ratified the Optional Protocol to the Convention against Torture and other Cruel, Inhuman or Degrading Treatment or Punishment (OPCAT) in 2003, promising to safeguard the dignity of all people deprived of their liberty in the UK. As part of this process, in 2009, the UK government created a National Preventative Mechanism (NPM)[2] to monitor the treatment and conditions of all people in detention. While multiple organisations make up the NPM of the UK, HMIP is the organising body and one of two organisations responsible for monitoring immigration removal centres.[3] In their role within the NPM, HMIP monitor the treatment of those detained in removal centres and pass on this information to the relevant institutions, authorities, and the state to ensure the dignity of those detained are upheld (Feldman, 2000).

Within immigration removal centres themselves, dignity is referenced during the initial statement of purpose:

> The purpose of detention centres shall be to provide for the secure but humane accommodation of detained persons in a relaxed regime with as much freedom of movement and association as possible consistent with maintaining a safe and secure environment, and to encourage and assist detained persons to make the most productive use of their time whilst respecting in particular their **dignity** and right to individual expression.
>
> *(Home Office, 2001)*

This use of human rights as the basis for standards and expectations for removal centres appears, on the face of it, both justified and promising in terms of ensuring dignified conditions. However, the theoretical bent of much academic literature and the legislation presented here do not explicate what it means or feels like when dignity is not respected. This book focuses on the experience of women who have spent time in immigration detention, and their perceptions of their treatment.

Therefore, I turn now to a variant of dignity known as 'social dignity' that is found in the field of health and social care and which is concerned with the lived experience and consequences of violations to a person's dignity.

The health and social care scholars I focus on in this book are concerned with the consequences of dignified conduct. Their work centres on the treatment of individuals or groups, and the effects of respecting or failing to respect their value as human beings. With this focus on outcomes, they provide a definition of dignity that links the concept clearly to everyday life and experience (see, for example, Chilton, 2006; Jacobson, 2007, 2009, 2010; Mann, 1998). The difference between social and human dignity in a practical sense is that this research predominantly focuses on nursing care and individuals' interactions with institutions of care, in real-life situations, whereby definitions of dignity are operationalised. Being treated as a human is broken down into actions and behaviours, such as 'I am treated as a person when a nurse uses my name.' Drawing on the scholarship of legal ethics theorist Nussbaum (1997) and public health academic Mann (1998), health academic Chilton summarises the difference between the rights drawn from human dignity and social dignity as a focus on claims and obligations and the suffering related to experience when obligations are not met. Dignity, she suggests, is a 'dynamic sense of worth that is socially and politically mediated' (Chilton, 2006). In her review of dignity and health, health scientist Jacobson (2007) defines social dignity as grounded in human dignity, differing only in terms of its tangibility. Social dignity, she argues, can be granted or denied to individuals by others. Being allowed or deprived of social dignity affects one's feelings of self-worth: 'Self-respect, self-esteem, pride', and 'confidence and self-assurances' (Jacobson, 2010). This definition designates dignity as a subjective concept, as feelings of self-worth can only be subjective and contextual.

Social definitions rely on the same underlying normative view as the literature on human dignity that individuals should be treated in a way that respects them, but it goes further than these fields by exploring the consequences of violations or promotions. It is in the articulation of what happens when respect is or is not granted that the scholarship in health sciences is most useful. Both Jacobson (2007, 2009, 2010) and Mann (1998) link dignity with experience and consequences, revealing the impact of treating patients with or without the humanity they expect. These works and others describe negative long-term social, physical, and mental health outcomes for individuals who have suffered from prolonged violations to their dignity. Similarly, when the worth of someone is respected, they can experience increased feelings of self-worth and motivation (Madan, 1992; Mann et al., 1994; Miller and Keys, 2001; Pleschberger, 2007).

Violations of dignity

Both Jacobson (2007, 2009, 2010) and Mann (1998) focus on what they refer to as violations of dignity, because, they say, these have a greater impact on the person than factors which promote dignity. Violations occur when actions towards an individual or group are so poor that those affected are not able to understand or justify their treatment. Human interactions are usually interpretable, however awful they may be. I may snap in anger because I am frustrated with my own work, a friend may ignore my calls because they are tired of hearing me complain about it. In both, the unwelcome interaction can be explained; there is a narrative with cause and effect.

It is when actions are morally incomprehensible that they offend the dignity of others. This is because there is no justification other than 'that person doesn't believe I am worthy/deserving/human,' and thus their actions violate our underlying sense of worth (Stoecker, 2011). Violations distort the normative moral relationship between individuals, corrupting what might be seen as an inherent baseline trust between human beings where we are all equal in rights (Maier, 2011; Neal, 2014). To help explain the concept of dignity violations ethics, philosopher Ralf Stoecker turns to the Holocaust, describing the example of Nazis forcing Jewish citizens to scrub pavements to help explain. He suggests that it was not the physical duress, or the fear, that violated their dignity, but rather it was the humiliation of being forced into such labour (Stoecker, 2003, 2011). The Holocaust is an extreme example of the consequences of not respecting the worth of humans, but also an important one to reflect upon. It starkly illuminates damage done when the dignity of populations is violated deliberately and on a mass scale. The violation to humanity through humiliation and dehumanisation of the Jewish population is what made the Holocaust unique and horrifying (Margalit and Motzkin, 2006) and what led to the human rights legislations discussed above (McCrudden, 2008).

Offences to human worth do not have to be as calculated or large as those witnessed during the Holocaust to have a negative effect on people. Violations to dignity can and do occur on a more everyday level. Their impacts vary, but are typically interpreted as a deviation from normal or expected treatment or behaviour. Jacobson (2009, 2010) and Mann (1998) found that examples of offence were readily recalled by individuals, even if they had occurred many years prior. Upon recalling such incidents, people 're-lived' their experiences and emotions as though they were recent (Mann, 1998). Some examples used by Jacobson are interactions such as when a person feels they are condescended, or talked down to, when they are forced into dependence, or when they are deliberately and unduly excluded from something. What violates one person's sense of dignity may not offend another; there will always be differences due to gender, culture, religion, age, and any other human variance (Feldman, 1999; Jacelon et al., 2004; Saltus and Pithara, 2014). The impacts of a transgression of someone's dignity, however, appear more analogous throughout academic literature, and the crux of the offence is that the person believes they have been wronged.

Jacobson describes a cycle of impact when a contravention of dignity has occurred. Take as an example an academic presenting a paper to their department. On conclusion, the head of their department stands and begins to criticise this work, unfairly and personally, perhaps suggesting the academic is foolish. Initially the academic will suffer from immediate emotional responses. They feel hurt or embarrassed in front of their peer group. These painful emotions will often be accompanied by others such as a sense of disbelief, powerlessness, and frustration as the academic finds it difficult to justify why their head of department has chosen this moment to criticise their work and intelligence so venomously. This stage in the cycle of impact is crucial, as it is where the offence to dignity is either lasting or fleeting. For the violation to only have a short-term effect, the offence needs to be rectified.

In this example, the academic's peers could promote the dignity of their colleague with positive reinforcement. The academic may be told that their work was in fact good and that they were intelligent and respected. Alternatively, if the violation remains un-remedied, such as if the colleagues remain silent and do nothing to defend their peer, the academic may suffer long-term emotional consequences. These include feelings of degradation, feeling wounded, worthless. Some people may also feel humiliated, angry or resentful, isolated, or insecure. Following these feelings are more the tangible effects of emotions including disempowerment, feelings of apathy, and ultimately depression.

Jacobson found consequences that went even further than disempowerment, apathy, and depression, where participants experienced substantial personal losses. A number of people in her study were marginalised from society in some way, through homelessness, illness, or similar, and many of these individuals reported loss of self-respect and loss of self-worth related to ongoing transgressions against their sense of dignity. Consequently, many of these individuals underwent a transformation of self, and a loss of social status and moral standing. The ultimate consequences of these losses could be seen in their long-term social and physical situations. These included social isolation, marginalisation, 'learned helplessness,' and chronically poor physical and mental health (Jacobson, 2009, 2010). Negative outcomes are particularly likely when someone is exposed to ongoing violations over time or when those affected are particularly vulnerable. That is to say, people are most adversely affected, when the person treating them occupies a position of power and authority (Chilton, 2006; Jacobson, 2009, 2010; Mann et al., 1994).

Dignity promotion

In the example offered above, where the dignity of an academic is offended during a presentation to their peers, I show how transgressions can be rectified through promotion. Dignity promotions are the inverse of violations. Promotions elevate feelings of self-worth, self-respect, and self-efficacy where violations relate to lessening of these same aspects of the self (Jacobson, 2009, 2010). Enhancements to an individual's feelings of worth are not as readily recalled by people as violations appear to be (Jacobson, 2009, 2010; Mann, 1998). However, Jacobson found that participants were eager to offer suggestions for the promotion of dignity for future practice. It is notable that most factors she believed would encourage dignity are often the antonyms of violations to dignity. For example, the antonym of the exclusion suggested as a violation of dignity, is deliberate and careful inclusion, or, rather than being forced into dependence, an individual is helped to be autonomous.

Returning to literature on the Holocaust, dignity promotions are shown to have played an important role in individuals' ability to survive dehumanising treatment in concentration camps. In her doctoral dissertation on the effects of trauma on the identity of Holocaust survivors, Lorelei Provost describes how men and women reinforced each other's sense of dignity in the camps. Through their accounts Provost describes how people maintained a sense of community: 'We were filthy, unwashed … we still said "please" and "thank you," we remained a functioning society' (Provost, 2015: 124). Through the narratives in Provost's work, individuals can be seen to be using discipline in their politeness to feel 'normal,' and courteous to their peers, while maintaining presence by maintaining a functioning society. Similar parallels can be drawn from other literature relating to Holocaust survivors where dignity has been maintained through resistance during their internment and managed post-liberation through advocacy and empowerment (Margalit and Motzkin, 2006; Provost, 2015; Schwartz Lee, 1988).

The enhancement of dignity is more likely if people are in a position of confidence, self-assurance, and hope. When coupled with a promoting actor who is compassionate, honest, open, and with clear good intentions, the effect is further realised (Chilton, 2006; Jacobson, 2009, 2010; Mann, 1998). In addition, trust, empathy reciprocity, and rapport between supporters and individuals are also conducive to the enhancement of an individuals' dignity, as are settings which promote humane circumstances, accessibility, and transparency (Jacobson, 2009, 2010).

There is an important relationship between dignity violations or promotions and the way in which people view themselves, and this is because an individual's sense of dignity is, at least in part, derived from social interaction. There are two elements to how someone assesses their sense of dignity, described as dignity-of-self and dignity-in-relation. Dignity-of-self is a confidence and integrity in an individual's own sense of self-respect and self-worth. Dignity-in-relation is the way in which this sense of self-respect and self-worth is supported and reflected by the collective behaviour of the community (Jacobson, 2009; Mann, 1998). Dignity-of-self then is determined by whether someone is treated with the respect they would expect from another person and therefore by dignity-in-relation.

The concepts of dignity-of-self and dignity-in-relation have their roots in symbolic interactionist perspectives. Founded by sociologists Cooley (1902) and Mead (1934), symbolic interactionism is based in the premise that our sense of self is developed through social experiences and interactions. Like dignity-of-self and dignity-in-relation, the self-described by Cooley and Mead has two elements; the 'I' and the 'Me.' The 'I' continuously perceives the environment surrounding it, focusing on the reaction of others to its own behaviour. The 'Me' internalises the reaction of others and changes their behaviour to reflect what is observed. This behaviour can be seen most obviously in young children, who when tripping over will often react based on the feedback of those around them. The concerned face of a parent will more often than not draw a cry, while a smiling face may elicit giggles.

Humans are continually assessing their internal dialogue based on the stimuli in their social environment. How people feel about themselves changes over time, based on the continued stimulus and reactions presented to them in society. Dignity-in-relation and dignity-of-self work in the same way. Dignity-in-relation is the 'I' where an individual assesses the behaviour of the community around them and whether it reflects the dignified behaviour that would be expected towards a human. Dignity-of-self will then react to the experience and internalise the reaction, either positively if dignity is upheld, 'I am worthy of dignity,' or negatively if dignity is not, 'I am not worthy of dignity.'

How dignified someone feels relates the impact of reduced self-esteem and self-worth. In psychology a relationship between self-esteem, mood, and well-being is well established (Argyle, 2001; Beck, 1967; Campbell, 1981; Cheng and Furnham, 2003; Wilson, 1967). In their statistical analyses, psychologists Helen Cheng and Adrian Furnham (2003) explored interactions between self-esteem and depression or happiness and found relationships with higher levels of self-esteem were related to higher indicators of happiness, while lower levels of self-esteem were related to higher indicators of depression. Further to this, a relationship between self-perception and health is also well recognised in psychological literature (Marmot, 2003; Salovey et al., 1998, 2000; Sennett, 2003). In particular, in their discussions of health and emotions, social psychologist Peter Salovey and colleagues (Salovey et al., 1998, 2000) have linked negative self-beliefs with negative emotional states which, in turn, are related to weakened immune systems.

Dignity, social and healthcare, and prisons

The consequences of respecting or not respecting someone's dignity are difficult to find in academic literature on law or moral philosophy, where, instead, scholars have tended to focus on defining dignity and the rights associated with these classifications (Mann, 1998). It is for this reason that I turn to other disciplines to support my argument for exploring the outcomes for women who have spent time in removal centres, and how these relate to dignity.

The first example of dignity and consequences in academic literature comes from research with homeless populations. In their study of 100 female heads of homeless households, for example, sociologists Seltser and Miller (1993) found dignity to be an unexpected but wide-ranging theme throughout their research. They conceptualised dignity as self-worth or inner worth, with dignified treatment defined as conduct that recognises the worth of an individual. In this study, the women's sense of self-worth was dependent on their ability to feel they were able to carry themselves with dignity, and also to be treated with respect. Seltser and Miller also found that for a woman to maintain her sense of self-worth, she must be able to validate her own internal sense of living with dignity and be treated in accordance with this lifestyle in her environment. For example, an individual must both believe they are worthy of respect and be treated with the associated respect to maintain feelings of self-worth. If only one element is present, such as if someone believes they should be treated with humanity, but they are treated with indifference by another person or organisation, this is when doubts over self-worth appear.

Seltser and Miller (1993) found that women who were not treated with dignity experienced feelings of worthlessness, passivity, and depression. These findings were supported by later research from Miller and Keys (2001), who developed the findings of Seltser and Miller further, focusing their research on dignity and homeless groups. Miller and Keys operationalised their research using their earlier counterparts' conceptualisation of dignity as internally and externally validating, asking participants which aspects of homelessness either validated or invalidated their sense of self-worth. The findings of this research reflect the taxonomy of dignity violations and promotions presented earlier in this chapter.

Dignity, for the men and women in Miller and Keys study, was validated when they were treated as individuals, as human beings, and when they felt they were a valued member of a group. Their feelings of self-worth were also bolstered when adequate resources were made available to them that met their basic survival needs, but also that helped participants to become self-sufficient. In the alternative, dignity was invalidated when men and women felt dehumanised or infantilised, or treated in a discriminatory manner based on their status as a homeless person. Similarly, participants felt their dignity was undermined when they received poor levels of service, such as being made to wait for long periods in queues or when the environment in which they were seeking help was negative; if homeless shelters were unclean or maintained poorly, for example. Unfairness in treatment and arbitrary or overzealous use of rules were also highlighted as potential transgressions of dignity.

It is in their account of the consequences of dignified treatment, where the work of Miller and Keys (2001b) adds most value to this book. They asked participants about how it felt when their dignity was validated or otherwise. As in the research by Jacobson (2010) and Mann and colleagues (1994), they found that responses to dignity violations were more readily recalled than promotions; however, the women and men in Miller and Keys' study readily divulged that validation of their dignity helped them to feel more confident, happier, and increased their feelings of self-worth. It also encouraged participants to self-motivate, improve themselves, and help others. When dignity was invalidated, respondents reported feeling worthless, feeling bad about themselves, and feeling angry and depressed. Further research on the subject of dignity and homelessness conducted by Hoffman and Coffey (2008) developed thinking on the consequences of disrespecting one's self-worth, illustrating that some men and women chose to 'opt out' of the homeless care system as a means to maintain their dignity and assert their sense of agency. Hoffman and Coffey also replicated many of the findings of Miller and Keys (2001), particularly focusing on their participants' experiences of objectification and infantilisation.

Dignity is a common concept in healthcare provision, both in the UK and overseas. In the UK it is a defining characteristic in multiple care standards, frameworks, and benchmarking reports. See, for example, the NHS plan (NHS, 2000), the NHS framework for older people (DoH, 2001), and the NHS essence of care (DoH, 2010). Academically there are multifaceted research projects on the implementation of dignity in care, all of which point to the importance of treating patients in a way that respects their sense of self-worth. These facets are typically directed at the ideas of treating patients with a common humanity, with respect for their individuality, and for the privacy and autonomy of men and women in care.

In the healthcare research both patients and those who care for them recognise that to treat someone as less than human is a violation of dignity (Gallagher and Seedhouse, 2002; Geller et al., 2015; Haddock, 1996; Henry et al., 2015; Skorpen et al., 2014). The notion of treating patients in care with a common humanity stems from the concept of human dignity described earlier, based on the underlying assumption that by virtue of being human, all individuals are owed a certain level of respect. In their study into dignity in intensive care units,

Henry and her colleagues (2015) focused on treatment with humanity. They suggest ensuring patients are not objectified, by ensuring they are referred to by name, rather than labelled and referred to by their illness or bed number, or discussed as though they are unable to hear or understand.

Respect for privacy was similarly referenced as humane treatment. In their research with patients and their relatives from hospital wards holding older patients, health scholars Gallagher and Seedhouse (2002) report how patients who are left uncovered or exposed during examinations feel embarrassment, degradation, and depression. Henry and colleagues (2015) suggest individuals hold expectations of privacy related to their bodies, and the intrusion of others without adequate permissions or discretion is linked to feelings of vulnerability and shame.

Part of treating men and women with shared humanity, requires an appreciation of them as individuals. Individualised dignity is based on the recognition that people develop their own life narratives and roles (Henry et al., 2015). A failure to respect the desires and preferences of an individual, is linked to a decline in the ability of people to maintain their personal identity throughout medical treatment and care. As a result, their sense of worth can be weakened (Coventry, 2006; Gennip et al., 2013; Matiti and Trorey, 2004).

The salience of autonomy and independence is another important theme in much of healthcare literature. Autonomy here refers to peoples' ability to control their situation within the limits of their medical situation. In their study, Gallagher and Seedhouse (2002) found the dignity of patients was threatened when they were treated as though they were children. Similarly, not sufficiently recognising the ability of patients to make decisions related to their treatment or general care can chip away at their independence and thus dignity (Gallagher and Seedhouse, 2002; Geller et al., 2015; Gennip et al., 2013; Henry et al., 2015).

Healthcare research on the impact of dignified treatment is further investigated in relation to the more sombre topic of dignity in death. This research shows that efforts to sustain dignity in dying, with an emphasis on making the individual feel valued, can ameliorate the symptoms of terminal illness and provide comfort to those nearing death (Brown, Johnston, and Östlund, 2011; Chochinov, 2002; Chochinov, Hack, McClement, Kristjanson, and Harlos, 2002; Johnson, 1998; Madan, 1992; Mathiews, 2010; Östlund, Brown, and Johnston, 2012; Pleschberger, 2007; Thompson and Chochinov, 2008). As with care for the unwell, when nursing men and women at the end of their lives, literature suggests that respect for privacy, individual beliefs, and culture are fundamental in the creation of a peaceful and comfortable death for both the dying and their families (Hemati et al., 2016).

The available literature on healthcare and dignity also suggests consequences that go beyond a loss of self-worth. Being treated with less respect than someone should be as a human can generate a build-up of chronic and acute stress. Over time this stress can become embodied and experienced as physical and mental health problems, such as those exemplified by men and women both in the immigration detention research and that of those released to the community (Chilton, 2006; Jacobson, 2007; Mann, 1998; Mann et al., 1994; Mann and Gruskin, 1995; Marmot and Wilkinson, 2006).

Prisons are the institutions that are most comparable with immigration removal centres in the UK. Fundamentally, individuals within both institutions are deprived of their liberty, albeit for very different reasons. A number of removal centres have also been built to prison specifications, staff are often former prison officers, and a great deal of management and operational language is directly lifted from prisons (Bosworth, 2012, 2014). It would then be difficult to write a well-rounded analysis of dignity and immigration detention without referring to prisons.

A rehabilitative focus for prisons began during the latter part of the 18th century (Van Zyl Smit and Snacken, 2009). This movement represented a substantial shift from the physical punishment (Foucault, 1977). Following the Second World War, the focus moved further towards human rights with the introduction of the UDHR and the additional resolutions and principles stated earlier in this chapter. It is without doubt that this focus on rights has driven improvements in prison conditions in the UK (Easton, 2013; Van Zyl Smit and Snacken, 2009), and much debate continues to be heard on prisoners' rights here (Lazarus, 2004). The prison service itself championed a 'decency agenda' from the 1990s, asserting that the treatment of prisoners with humanity was their underlying principle (Coyle, 2003).

According to Van Zyl Smit and Snacken (2009), the recognition of prisoner rights goes some way to square the power imbalances between prisoners and prison staff. In doing so, they argue, rights may reduce the 'pains of imprisonment,' as defined by in the classic work of Sykes (1958): Lack of autonomy and a sense of self and personal security (Van Zyl Smit and Snacken, 2009). A parallel can drawn here between the definition of dignity expressed within Jacobson's taxonomy of dignity violations and promotions. Prisoners are at less risk of *assault*, *restriction*, *objectification*, and *intrusion*, amongst many other violations. With a focus on rights and rehabilitation, prisoners are also more likely than before to experience *enrichment*, *recognition*, and *achievement* while incarcerated, thus improving their sense of self-worth and ability to function as an active member of the community once released.

In practice, the experience of prisoners will vary between institutions, even when prisons serve similar functions (Liebling, 2011). Two category C training prisons, for example, can and do differ substantially on measures relating to quality of life of prisoners, or during inspections based on human rights expectations. In her work on the quality of life in prisons, Liebling (2004) discusses prison qualities and their impact on the prisoners who are detained there. Liebling does not focus on dignity directly; rather, she discusses the counterparts of dignity: respect and humanity. Treatment which recognised the dignity of prisoners was evidenced by the definition of respect drawn from prisoners who participated in the research. Respect was important to the prisoners in Liebling's study, with participants able to provide clear examples of treatment with the concept. Liebling links humanity to dignity in a similar way, defining the concept of humanity as respect for another person's dignity. Again, humanity was an important concept for prisoners, who linked the term to being treated as a human, rather than 'prisoner' or 'criminal.' On the whole, Liebling concludes that outcomes for prisoners are linked to the moral performance of prisons. Her conclusions include her measures for humanity and respect and include a range of other measures,[4] of which many can also be related in some way to dignity. Poor moral performance is then related, by Liebling, to negative outcomes including heightened levels of psychological distress, anxiety, depression, and rates of suicide of prisoners (Liebling, 2004).

In another measure of humanity in prison, Coyle (2003) suggests there are four key elements required to ensure inmates are treated as human. The first, he determines, is the preservation of human dignity. Coyle suggests the acknowledgement of the dignity of prisoners prevents their ill treatment. To be treated with dignity, he states, all matters of personal integrity must be relevant, but particularly those of an intimate nature such as personal hygiene, appearance, and bodily functions. The importance of this can be found where 'history has shown time and again that it is much easier to ill-treat and brutalise people who are dirty and unkempt, who smell unpleasant and who are dressed in stigmatising clothes' (Coyle, 2003: 36). Coyle also calls for the individuality of prisoners to be respected, citing basic human empathy as a tool to consider if the treatment of an inmate is suitable for that individual's situation. Treating prisoners as human in this way protects them from feeling like objects or 'just another prisoner' with little self-worth.

Coyle argues that in order to treat prisoners as human, they must be encouraged and supported to develop their personal responsibility and development (Coyle, 2003). This work aligns with the dignity promotions suggested by Jacobson, where someone's self-worth and esteem can be built through the enhancement of accomplishment and opportunities to contribute to society (Jacobson, 2010). Summarising the worth of promoting personal development, Coyle makes clear links between dignity and self-respect, as 'respect for the inherent dignity of the human being includes a respect for that person's capacity to grow, to develop, to do things that allow them to increase their self-respect' (Coyle, 2003: 41).

Another important aspect which relates to dignity and prison is that of stigma. Imprisonment is a key identifier of a 'spoiled identity' as presented by Goffman in his founding works on stigma (Goffman, 1963). On top of the possible violations to dignity described above, prisoners must also manage the consequences of being labelled as 'criminal' on release (LeBel, 2012; Moore, Stuewig, and Tangney, 2013; Moran, 2012). The stigma of criminal presents additional challenges to the maintenance of dignity as opportunities for dignity promotion and thus self-esteem and self-worth are diminished (LeBel, 2012; Moore, Stuewig, and Tangney, 2013; Moran, 2012). Likewise, former prisoners must manage the effects of vicarious stigmatisation on their families. In the work of Condry, families of offenders feel vicarious shame as a result of their loved one's label as a serious offender and prisoner (Condry, 2007). As will become apparent in this book, women who have spent time in immigration detention must similarly manage the label of prisoner, often without committing a criminal offence.

The relevance of dignity in immigration detention

Earlier in this chapter, I presented the human rights legislations and protections that relate to people in immigration detention in the UK, and I suggest that using human rights as the basis for standards and expectations for removal centres appear to be justified and promising for the protection of dignity in immigration detention. However, investigation into the treatment of individuals in removal centres in the UK appears to be in conflict with these works. In 2013, four years after the implementation of the OPCAT, HMIP's annual report referred to the removal centres inspected that year as 'safe, but degrading' (HMIP, 2013: 66). Annual reports from the same organisation summarise removal centres as places which are safe, relative to other places of inspection, such as prisons. However, within the reports, the Chief Inspector continues to highlight concerns for the welfare of people in detention linked to issues surrounding fairness and casework linked to a lack of care from the Home Office (HMIP, 2014a, 2015).

Since 2011, cases brought before the High Court of Justice in England have ruled that the treatment of six men and women while detained in immigration detention was inhuman and degrading (Royal Courts of Justice:; *BA v Secretary of State for the Home Department*, 2011; *S v Secretary of State for the Home Department*, 2011; *D v Secretary of State for the Home Department*, 2012; *MD, R (On the Application Of) v Secretary of State for the Home Department*, 2014; *R. (on the application of S) v Secretary of State for the Home Department*, 2014). Each had suffered from mental illness, with the latest case Judgment finding that detention caused major depression with psychotic features for a young Guinean woman (*MD, R (On the Application Of) v Secretary of State for the Home Department*, 2014).

In addition, in their investigation into the death of an Alois Dvorak, an elderly man detained under immigration powers, the Prisons and Probation Ombudsman (PPO) suggested this man's treatment also amounted to inhuman and degrading treatment (PPO, 2015). These findings illustrate that in the case of immigration detention, the UK has repeatedly breached Article 3 of the European Convention of Human Rights 'No one shall be subjected to torture or to inhuman or degrading treatment or punishment' (European Court of Human Rights, 1970). Most recently in Kate Lampard's (2016) independent investigation into the concerns about Yarl's Wood Immigration Removal Centre, failure to respect the privacy and dignity of the female residents of this centre was a common complaint.

The findings of the High Courts, Inspectorate of Prisons, and independent reviewers above suggest there are failings in the immigration removal estate in the UK. Such problems occur despite the ratification of human rights doctrine that respects the dignity of all humans, and notwithstanding regular, practical inspection of places of detention against human rights legislation. So, too, they occur, despite statements of intent from companies who run removal centres placing dignity as an important concept in the treatment of men and women in detention.

It is clear that parallels can be drawn between existing works on immigration detention and that of dignity theorists relating to dignified treatment in detention. The small amount of literature available suggests that the experiences of those in detention are poor and akin to violations of dignity described by social dignity theorists such as Jacobson (2007, 2009, 2010) and Mann (1998). Likewise, there is evidence of negative long-term social, physical, and mental health outcomes for this population (Bosworth, 2008; 2011; 2012; Bosworth and Kellezi, 2012; Steel et al., 2011; Coffey et al., 2010; Klein and Williams, 2012; Robjant et al., 2009; Griffin, 2009; Brotherton and Barrios, 2009; Miller, 2012; Schuster and Majidi, 2013), as per the consequences of offences to dignity presented in psychological, health, and social care literature.

The indefinite nature of detention in the UK is a key factor restricting the ability of individuals to direct their own lives. Indefinite detention deprives individuals of self-determination, autonomy, and the ability to plan for their future, which are believed to be necessities for living a dignified life (Griffiths, 2013; Jacobson, 2009; Nussbaum, 1997; Phelps, 2009). Those detained report institutional indifference, with a lack of access to legal advice and case workers – an example of diminishment, disregard, and contempt where people are treated as though they have no value (Bosworth, 2012; Bosworth and Kellezi, 2012; Griffiths, 2013, Phelps, 2009). Even when released from detention, people felt excluded and unwanted in the UK. It is also evident in the literature that individuals experience considerable social isolation, marginalisation, and learned helplessness post detention (Coffey et al., 2010; Klein and Williams, 2012; Steel et al., 2011). This appears to be the case for those that are both released and removed from detention.

People released from detention appeared to suffer from social isolation, often coupled with depression, stress, anxiety, and PTSD (Coffey et al., 2010; Steel et al., 2011). The ongoing restrictions for formerly detained men and women fulfil the criteria for continued violations of dignity even after detention. Under the conditions described above, individuals continue to experience restriction, dependence, and deprivation. The use of methods such as tagging and voucher systems are also expressive of a system of suspicion and vilification, where people are distrusted and treated as though they have committed bad acts and are made to appear threatening and dangerous.

Removed individuals were unprepared for their return and many found re-integration difficult. Many had limited access to funds or assets and were reliant on the charity of family members to survive (Brotherton and Barrios, 2009; Coffey et al., 2010; Golash-Boza, 2015; Griffin, 2009; Miller, 2012; Schuster and Majidi, 2013; Steel et al., 2011). The removal of men and women from the UK with little to no preparation demonstrates an indifference and disregard for the welfare of this population. It also leaves them in state of dependence and deprivation.

Defining dignity in this study

When conducting the research for this book, it was pertinent to use the definitions of dignity presented by the women in my study. I designed my interview schedules so that I would first ask women about their experiences in detention and since leaving the centres. To avoid leading participants, I avoided questions relating to dignity until I was convinced I had been told all that the women were willing to tell me about their lives. When I moved to the topic, I asked women to describe or define what they thought the word dignity meant. I had a range of ways I approached this issue, depending on how well the initial stages of the interview had progressed. This transition was easiest when women had used the term 'dignity' themselves and I could ask them what they meant by it. The transition was more difficult if language barriers were present, but this was not very common. I found most women were interested in the question and gave a good amount of thought to their answer. Following their definitions, and often as part of their description of dignity, many women provided concrete examples of a time when they were not treated with dignity during their stay in a removal centre, or once they had left. I was then able to ask them to reflect on their experiences of the immigration process considering their subjective interpretations of dignity.

Most of the women's accounts resonated with the taxonomy of dignity violations and promotions from Jacobson's work (2010) and health and social care literature on subjective dignity definitions (see, for example, Chilton, 2006; Miller and Keys, 2001). Many described key terms, such as 'humiliated,' and 'labelled,' which align directly. For example, Danielle,[5] a 65-year-old grandmother who I spoke with in detention complained, '[The Home Office] label, they label me they say somebody there is not a, is not of our thing, is something they touch unto me, not supposed to be in my way, when it's a label!'

In another example, Luciana, who had lived in Belfast with her British partner and daughter before she was arrested by immigration, described to me an instance where she claimed an officer had knocked the biscuit Luciana had reached for to the floor and then told her to pick up. I asked her how she felt when the officer did that, she replied: 'Horrible. Humiliated. Everybody was looking.' Others did not refer directly to a violation concept, such as labelling or humiliation, but their words were easily attributed to one. For example, Cassie, who I spoke with in immigration detention voiced the story of her first deportation.[6] In the following quote, I coded her experience as 'Intrusion': 'I couldn't go even to the toilet. Police, this woman, was to stand there when I'm peeing! Dignity is all taken away.' Other responses relating to dignity did not relate directly to the a priori coding frame based on Jacobson's work, and so I used grounded theory to add concepts and themes to my frame as I worked through interviews. For example, women regularly referred to feeling like a criminal. I spoke with Samantha when she was in detention, she described to me how being treated like a prisoner made her feel that she was not treated with dignity: 'Because that's the stigma they gave you. You are a criminal. Even though you know in yourself, I'm not a criminal. I only make a mistake.' I coded this example as criminalisation. Though the narrative described aspects of labelling which are covered by my a priori framework, the discussions relating to criminalisation had a particularly damaging effect on women's sense of dignity in this research that went beyond labelling on its own.

I facilitated two focus groups to assure myself that the frameworks I was using to code the research were recognisable to the population of women who were the subject of my book. The first was held immediately after I completed the work in detention. The second was conducted after my time in Jamaica, towards the end of the community fieldwork. I would have preferred to complete the second focus group after my period in the community was over; however, I was restricted by the timetable of the women's group who had agreed to participate.

I conducted the first group with approximately 30 participants at the women's group drop-in session. A large portion of those in this group had spent time in immigration detention. All were seeking asylum or had refugee status. I did not record the focus group, as I did not think it would be possible to gain full consent from the participants, especially as people came and went during the group. I also felt women would be more open without it. Instead, I created mind maps using large pieces of paper and marker pens. Mind maps are a visual method where a concept, usually a word, is drawn in the centre of a page and the author will then write down other words that are associated with the central concept. Mind maps allow creative associations to be made, which can assist researchers to explore definitions and connections of their participants (Buzan, 2003; Davies, 2011; Wheeldon and Faubert, 2009). During the session, the group and I worked together to complete mind maps with the central concepts of 'Dignity,' 'Feeling,' 'Dignity Promotion,' and 'Community.'

The information gathered in this way helped me to interpret the data I had already collected, by adding to the definitions provided by women during interviews. By the time I conducted the second focus group I was further along in my fieldwork, and so I was able to ask for feedback on my emerging interpretations of interview themes. For the second focus group, I utilised marker pens and paper again. However, this time I prepared in advance quotes from earlier interviews. I had interpreted each quote in advance, coding them based on the emerging definitions of dignity from data already collected. I did not share these with the group, instead asking them to tell me what they thought the quoted participant was trying to say. I found that the coding I had conducted already aligned with the interpretations provided by those who participated in the focus group. This feedback gave me confidence that my developing coding frame and themes were reflecting the narratives provided to me by the participants.

Following coding and analysis of interviews, and the focus groups I have just described, I could establish my own definition of dignity for use in this book. As such, considering the findings from this project, and the existing work on dignity, the definition used for this book is that dignity is a person's belief that they are worth something. The exploration of the concept is then the experiences of women in relation to the way in which they feel they should be treated as humans.

Conclusion

I suggest that the instruments used to measure dignity in detention are based on human rights and dignity as legislation rather than on dignity as the lived experience of people affected by immigration controls. While it is unrealistic to expect one inspecting body to identify and cure all violations to dignity within an institution, the poor conditions and the negative outcomes of immigration detention, described above, suggest there is a disjuncture between dignity as defined by legislation and the experience of those detained in removal centres. As Bosworth put it, 'a considerable gap remains between human rights theory and practice in Britain's immigration detention centres' (Bosworth, 2011: 181). If this disjuncture exists, then we are failing in our obligations to protect vulnerable populations both under international law and morally.

Notes

1 The tattoo is in fact an in-joke if you happen to be a fan of the Simpsons. The tattoo is a depiction of the picture Milhouse's dad creates in his attempt to draw 'Dignity' during a game of Pictionary. The scene it is drawn from is a surprisingly nuanced depiction of the challenges of defining dignity, and also the subjective nature of it.
2 For more information on the UK NPM, see the annual report (Human Rights Commission, 2015).
3 The second organisation responsible for monitoring immigration detention is the Independent Monitoring Board (IMB).
4 The full range of measures are respect, humanity, staff–prisoner relationships, support, fairness, order, safety, well-being, personal development, family contact, and decency.
5 The names of all participants in this book are pseudonyms to protect their privacy.
6 Cassie had been deported once before, returning to the UK after her life and that of her sister were threatened when militia found she was back in the country.

References

Argyle M (2001) *The Psychology of Happiness* (2nd ed.). London: Routledge.

Beck A (1967) *Depression: Causes and Treatment*. Philadelphia: University of Pennsylvania Press.

Birnbacher D (1996) Ambiguities in the concept of Menschenwurde. In: Bayertz K (ed.) *Sanctity of Life and Human Dignity*. Amsterdam: Kluwer Academic Publishers, pp. 107–121.

Bosworth M (2008) Immigration detention. *Criminal Justice Matters* 71(1): 24–25. https://doi.org/10.1080/09627250801937611.

Bosworth M (2011) Human rights and immigration detention in the United Kingdom. In: Dembour M-B and Kelly T (eds.) *Are Human Rights for Migrants? Critical Reflections on the Status of Irregular Migrants in Europe and the United States*. London: Routledge, pp. 165–183.

Bosworth M (2012) Subjectivity and identity in detention: Punishment and society in a global age. *Theoretical Criminology* 16(2): 123–140. https://doi.org/10.1177/1362480612441116.

Bosworth M (2014) *Inside Immigration Detention*. Oxford: Oxford University Press.

Bosworth M and Kellezi B (2012) Quality of life in detention: Results for MQLD questionnaire data collected in IRC Yarl's Wood, IRC Tinsley House, and IRC Brook House, August 2010 - Hune 2011. (February).

Brotherton DC and Barrios L (2009) Displacement and stigma: The social-psychological crisis of the deportee. *Crime, Media, Culture* 5(1): 29–55. https://doi.org/10.1177/1741659008102061.

Brown H, Johnston B and Ostlund U (2011) Identifying care actions to conserve dignity in end-of-life care. *British Journal of Community Nursing* 16(5): 238–245.

Buzan T (2003) The mind map book. In: *The Mind Map Book How to Use Radiant Thinking to Maximize Your Brains Untapped Potential*. Buzan Organization. https://doi.org/citeulike-article-id:960994.

Campbell A (1981) *The Sense of Well-Being in America: Recent Patterns and Trends*. New York: McGraw-Hill.

Cheng H and Furnham A (2003) Personality, self-esteem, and demographic predictions of happiness and depression. *Personality and Individual Differences* 34(6): 921–942. https://doi.org/10.1016/S0191-8869(02)00078-8.

Chilton M (2006) Developing a measure of dignity for stress-related health outcomes. *Health and Human Rights* 9(2): 208–233. https://doi.org/10.2307/4065408.

Chochinov HM (2002) Dignity-conserving care–A new model for palliative care: Helping the patient feel valued. *JAMA: The Journal of the American Medical Association* 287(17): 2253–2260.

Chochinov HM, Hack T, McClement S, Kristjanson L and Harlos M (2002) Dignity in the terminally ill: A developing empirical model. *Social Science and Medicine* 54(3): 433–443. https://doi.org/10.1016/S0277-9536(01)00084-3.

Coffey GJ, Kaplan I, Sampson RC and Tucci MM (2010) The meaning and mental health consequences of long-term immigration detention for people seeking asylum. *Social Science and Medicine* 70(12): 2070–2079. https://doi.org/10.1016/j.socscimed.2010.02.042.

Condry R (2007) *Families Shamed: The Consequences of Crime for Relatives of Serious Offenders*. Devon: Willan Publishing.

Cooley CH (1902) The social self - 1. The meaning of "I". In: *Human Nature and the Social Order*, pp. 136–178. https://doi.org/10.1093/mind/LXIV.253.122-b.

Coventry M (2006) Care with dignity: A concept analysis. *Journal of Gerontological Nursing* 32(5): 42–48.

Coyle A (2003) *Humanity in Prison; Questions of Definition and Audit*. London: International Centre for Prison Studies.

Dales RC (1977) A medieval view of human dignity. *Journal of the History of Ideals* 38(4): 557–572. http://ojs.libraries.psu.edu/index.php/phj/article/viewFile/21299/21068.

Davies M (2011) Concept mapping, mind mapping and argument mapping: What are the differences and do they matter? *Higher Education* 62(3): 279–301.

DoH (2001) *National Service Framework for Older People*. London: Department of Health.

DoH (2010) *Essence of Care*. London: Department of Health.

Donnelly J (1982) Human rights and human dignity: An analytic critique of non-western conceptions of human rights. *American Political Science Review* 76(2): 303–316.

Dupre C (2009) Unlocking human dignity: Towards a theory for the 21st century. *European Human Rights Law Review* 2: 190–206.

Easton S (2013) Protecting prisoners: The impact of international human rights law on the treatment of prisoners in the United Kingdom. *The Prison Journal* 93(4): 475–492. https://doi.org/10.1177/0032885513501025.

European Court of Human Rights (1970) *European Convention on Human Rights*. European Court of Human Rights, p. 56. https://doi.org/10.1093/iclqaj/21.4.795.

Feldman D (1999) Human dignity as a legal value: Part 1. *Public Law* (Winter): 682–702.

Feldman D (2000) Human dignity as a legal value: Part 2. *Public Law* (Spring): 61–76.

Foucault M (1977) *Discipline and Punish: The Birth of the Prison*. New York: Pantheon Books.

Gallagher A and Seedhouse D (2002) Dignity in care: The views of patients and relatives. *Nursing Times* 98(43): 38–41.

Geller G, Branyon E, Forbes L, Rushton CH, Beach MC, Aboumatar H and Sugarman J (2015) Health care professionals' perceptions and experiences of respect and dignity in the intensive care unit. *Narrative Inquiry in Bioethics* 5(1A): 27A–42A.

Gennip IE Van, Pasman HRW, Oosterveld-Vlug MG, Willems DL and Onwuteaka-Philipsen BD (2013) The development of a model of dignity in illness based on qualitative interviews with seriously ill patients. *International Journal of Nursing Studies* 50(8): 1080–1089. https://doi.org/10.1016/j.ijnurstu.2012.12.014.

Goffman I (1963) *Stigma: Notes on the Management of Spoiled Identity*. London: Penguin.

Golash-Boza T (2015) *Deported: Immigration Policing, Disposable Labour, and Global Capitalism*. New York: New York University Press.

Griffin CE (2009) Deportation and reintegration in the Caribbean and Latin America: Addressing the development–security paradox. In: Mcdonald WF (ed.) *Immigration, Crime and Justice: 13 (Sociology of Crime Law and Deviance)* (Vol. 13). Emerald Group Publishing, pp. 279–296. https://doi.org/10.1108/S1521-6136(2009)0000013018.

Griffiths M (2013) Living with uncertainty: Indefinite immigration detention. *Journal of Legal Anthropology* 1(3): 263–286. https://doi.org/10.4059/jla.2013.2616.

Guerra MD (2001) The affirmation of genuine human dignity. *The Journal of Markets and Morality* 4(2): 295–301.

Habermas J (2010) The concept of human dignity and the realistic Utopia of human rights. *Metaphilosophy* 41(4): 464–480. https://doi.org/10.1111/j.1467-9973.2010.01648.x.

Haddock J (1996) Towards further clarification of the concept "dignity". *Journal of Advanced Nursing* 24(5): 924–931.

Hemati Z, Ashouri E, Allahbakhshian M, Pourfarzad Z, Shirani F, Safazadeh S, Ziyaei M, Varzeshnejad M, Hashemi M and Taleghani F (2016) Dying with dignity: A concept analysis. *Journal of Clinical Nursing* 25(9–10): 1218–1228. https://doi.org/10.1111/jocn.13143.

Henry LM, Rushton C, Beach MC and Faden R (2015) Respect and dignity: A conceptual model for patients in the intensive care unit. *Narrative Inquiry in Bioethics* 5(1A): 5A–14A.

HMIP (2013) *HM Chief Inspector of Prisons for England and Wales Annual Report 2012–13*. London: HM Inspectorate of Prisons.

HMIP (2014a) *HM Chief Inspector of Prisons for England and Wales Annual Report 2013–14*. In Office. London: HM Inspectorate of Prisons.

HMIP (2014b) *National Preventative Mechanism*. London: HM Inspectorate of Prisons.

HMIP (2015) *HM Chief Inspector of Prisons for England and Wales Annual Report 2014–15*. London: HM Inspectorate of Prisons.

Hoffman L and Coffey B (2008) Dignity and indignation: How people experiencing homelessness view services and providers. *The Social Science Journal* 45(2): 207–222. https://doi.org/10.1016/j.soscij.2008.03.001.

Home Office (2001) *The Detention Centre Rules 2001, Statutory Instrument No. 238 Immigration*. London: Home Office.

Human Rights Commission (2015) *Monitoring Places of Detention 2015: Sixth Annual Report of the United Kingdom's National Preventive Mechanism* (6th ed., Issue April 2014). Human Rights Commission. http://www.scoop.co.nz/stories/PO1512/S00165/monitoring-places-of-detention-2015.

Jacelon CS, Assistant C-A, Connelly TW, Brown R, Rn B, Proulx K, Vo T and Jacelon C (2004) A concept analysis of dignity for older adults. *Journal of Advanced Nursing* 48(1): 76–83. https://doi.org/10.1111/j.1365-2648.2004.03170.x.

Jacobson N (2007) Dignity and health: A review. *Social Science and Medicine* 64(2): 292–302. https://doi.org/10.1016/j.socscimed.2006.08.039.

Jacobson N (2009) A taxonomy of dignity: A grounded theory study. *BMC International Health and Human Rights* 9: 3. https://doi.org/10.1186/1472-698X-9-3.

Jacobson N (2010) *Dignity and Health*. Nashville: Vanderbilt University Press.

Johnson JP (1971) Human dignity and the nature of society. *World Futures* 10(3): 213–248. https://doi.org/10.1080/02604027.1971.9971751.

Johnson PR (1998) An analysis of "dignity". *Theoretical Medicine and Bioethics* 19(4): 337–352.

Kant I (1996) Groundwork for the metaphysics of morals. In: *Practical Philosophy*, pp. 41–108. https://doi.org/10.1515/9783110204551.

Killmister S (2010) Dignity: Not such a useless concept. *Journal of Medical Ethics* 36(3): 160–164. https://doi.org/10.1136/jme.2009.031393.

Klein A and Williams L (2012) Immigration detention in the community: Research on the experiences of migrants released from detention centres in the UK. *Population, Space and Place* 18(6): 741–753. https://doi.org/10.1002/psp.1725.

Kolnai A (1976) Dignity. *Philosophy* 51(197): 251–271.

Korsgaard C (1992) Creating the kingdom of ends: Reciprocity and responsibility in personal relations. *Philosphical Perspectives* 6: 305–332. https://doi.org/10.2307/2214250.

Kraynak RP and Tinder G (2003) *In Defense of Human Dignity: Essays for Our Times*. Kraynak RP and Tinder G (eds.). Indiana: University of Notre Dame Press.

Lampard K (2016) *Independent Investigation into Concerns about Yarl's Wood Immigration Removal Centre*. (January).London: SERCO

Lazarus L (2004) *Contrasting Prisoners' Rights: A Comparative Examination of England and Germany*. Oxford: Oxford University Press.

LeBel T (2012) Invisible stripes? Formerly incarcerated persons' perceptions of stigma. *Deviant Behavior* 33(2): 89–107. https://doi.org/10.1080/01639625.2010.538365.

Liebling A (2004) *Prisons and their Moral Performance: A Study of Values, Quality and Prison Life*. Oxford: Oxford University Press.

Liebling A (2011) Moral performance, inhuman and degrading treatment and prison pain. *Punishment and Society* 13(5): 530–550. https://doi.org/10.1177/1462474511422159.

Madan TN (1992) Dying with dignity. *Social Science and Medicine* 35(4): 425–432. https://doi.org/10.1016/0277-9536(92)90335-N.

Maier A (2011) Torture. In: Kaufmann P, Kuch H, Neuhauser C and Webster E (eds.) *Humiliation, Degradation, Dehumanization: Human Dignity Violated*. New York: Springer, pp. 101–117.

Mann J (1998) Dignity and health: The UDHR's revolutionary first article. *Health and Human Rights* 3(2): 31–38.

Mann J, Gostin L, Gruskin S, Brennan T, Lazzarini Z and Fineberg HV (1994) Health and human rights. *Health and Human Rights* 1(1): 6–23. https://doi.org/10.2307/4065260.

Mann J and Gruskin S (1995) Women's health and human rights: Genesis of the health and human rights movement. *Health and Human Rights* 1(4): 309–312. https://doi.org/10.2307/4065245.

Margalit A and Motzkin G (2006) The uniqueness of the Holocaust. *Philosophy and Public Affairs* 25(1): 65–83. https://doi.org/10.1111/j.1088-4963.1996.tb00076.x.

Marmot M (2003) Self esteem and health. *BMJ (Clinical Research Ed)* 327(7415): 574–575. https://doi.org/10.1136/bmj.327.7415.574.

Marmot M and Wilkinson R (2006) *Social Determinants of Health*. Marmot M and Wilkinson R (eds.). 2nd ed. Oxford University Press.

Mathiews AK (2010) Death with dignity. *Creative Nursing* 16(4): 185–187. https://doi.org/10.1136/jme.28.4.255.

Matiti RM and Trorey G (2004) Perceptual adjustment levels: Patients' perception of their dignity in the hospital setting. *International Journal of Nursing Studies* 41(7): 735–744. https://doi.org/10.1016/j.ijnurstu.2004.02.008.

McCrudden C (2008) Human dignity and judicial interpretation of human rights. *European Journal of International Law* 19(4): 655–724. https://doi.org/10.1093/ejil/chn043.

Mead GH (1934) *Mind, Self, and Society: From the Standpoint of a Social Behaviorist*. Morris CW (ed.). Chicago: University of Chicago Press.

Mendes S (2012) *Skyfall*. California: Metro-Goldwyn-Mayer (MGM) and Columbia Pictures.

Meyer MJ (1989) Dignity, rights, and self-control*. *Ethics* 99(3): 520–534. https://doi.org/10.1086/293095.

Miller A (2012) Deportation as a process of irreversible transformation. *Journal of Ethnic and Migration Studies* 38(May): 131–146. https://doi.org/10.1080/1369183X.2012.640024.

Miller AB and Keys CB (2001) Understanding dignity in the lives of homeless persons. *American Journal of Community Psychology* 29(2): 331–354. https://doi.org/10.1023/A:1010399218126.

Misztal BA (2012) The idea of dignity: Its modern significance. *European Journal of Social Theory* 16(1): 101–121. https://doi.org/10.1177/1368431012449237.

Moore K, Stuewig J and Tangney J (2013) Jail inmates' perceived and anticipated stigma: Implications for post-release functioning. *Self and Identity* 12(5): 527–547. https://doi.org/10.1080/15298868.2012.702425.

Moran D (2012) Prisoner reintegration and the stigma of prison time inscribed on the body. *Punishment and Society* 14(5): 564–583. https://doi.org/10.1177/1462474512464008.

Morsink J (2000) *Pennsylvania Studies in Human Rights: Universal Declaration of Human Rights: Origins, Drafting and Intent*. Philadelphia: University of Pennsylvania Press.

Neal M (2014) Respect for human dignity as 'substantive basic norm'. *International Journal of Law in Context* 10(1): 26–46. https://doi.org/10.1017/S1744552313000359.

NHS (2000) *The NHS Plan: A Plan for Investment, a Plan for Reform*. London: National Health Service.

Nordenfelt L (2004) The varieties of dignity. *Health Care Analysis: HCA: Journal of Health Philosophy and Policy* 12(2): 69–81; discussion 83–89. https://doi.org/10.1023/B:HCAN.0000041183.78435.4b.

Nussbaum M (1997) Capabilities and human rights. *Fordham Law Review* 66: 273–300. Available from: https://ir.lawnet.fordham.edu/flr/vol66/iss2/

Ombudsman P (2015) *A Report by the Prisons and Probation Ombudsman Nigel Newcomen CBE.* (February).

Östlund U, Brown H and Johnston B (2012) Dignity conserving care at end-of-life: A narrative review. *European Journal of Oncology Nursing* 16(4): 353–367. https://doi.org/10.1016/j.ejon.2011.07.010.

Phelps J (2009) *Detained Lives: The Real Cost of Indefinite Immigration Detention.* (January).

Pleschberger S (2007) Dignity and the challenge of dying in nursing homes: The residents' view. *Age and Ageing* 36(2): 197–202. https://doi.org/10.1093/ageing/afl152.

Provost L (2015) *Understanding the Effects of Trauma on Identity: Voices of Holocaust Survivors.* New York: New York University.

Robjant K, Robbins I and Senior V (2009) Psychological distress amongst immigration detainees: A cross-sectional questionnaire study. *The British Journal of Clinical Psychology* 48(Pt 3): 275–286. https://doi.org/10.1348/014466508X397007.

Rosen M (2012) *Dignity: It's History and Meaning.* Cambridge: Harvard University Press.

Rothhaar M (2010) Human dignity and human rights in bioethics: The Kantian approach. *Medicine, Health Care, and Philosophy* 13(3): 251–257. https://doi.org/10.1007/s11019-010-9249-0.

Rowling J (2007) Book 7 - Harry Potter and the deathly hallows. *Fiction*: 1–501. https://doi.org/10.1353/bcc.2007.0672.

Royal Courts of Justice (2011) *BA v Secretary of State for the Home Department* (2011). EWHC 2748 (Admin),

Royal Courts of Justice (2011) *S v Secretary of State for the Home Department* (2011).EWHC 2120 (Admin)

Royal Courts of Justice (2012) *HA Nigeria v Secretary of State for the Home Department.* EWHC 979 (Admin).

Royal Courts of Justice (2012) *D v Secretary of State for the Home Department* [2012] EWHC 2501 (Admin)

Royal Courts of Justice (2014) *MD, R (on the Application of) v Secretary of State for the Home Department* (2014). EWHC 2249 (Admin)

Royal Courts of Justice (2014) *R. (on the Application of S) v Secretary of State for the Home Department* (2014). EWHC 50 (Admin).

Salovey P, Rothman AJ, Detweiler JB and Steward WT (2000) Emotional states and physical health. *The American Psychologist* 55(1): 110–121. https://doi.org/10A037//0003-O66X.55.1.110.

Salovey P, Rothman A and Rodin J (1998) Health behaviour. In: Gilbert T, Fiske S and Lindzey G (eds.) *The Handbook of Social Psychology.* 4th ed. New York: McGraw-Hill, pp. 633–683.

Saltus R and Pithara C (2014) A sense of dignity in later life: A qualitative study on the views of older women migrants from minoritised backgrounds. *Quality in Ageing and Older Adults* 15(1): 21–33. https://doi.org/10.1108/QAOA-06-2013-0016.

Schuster L and Majidi N (2013) What happens post-deportation? The experience of deported Afghans. *Migration Studies* 1(2): 221–240. https://doi.org/10.1093/migration/mns011.

Schwartz Lee B (1988) Holocaust survivors and internal strengths. *Journal of Humanistic Psychology* 28(1): 67–96.

Seltser BJ and Miller DE (1993) *Homeless Families: The Struggle for Dignity.* Champaign: University of Illinois Press.

Sennett R (2003) *Respect in a World of Inequality.* New York: W.W. Norton and Company Inc.

Sensen O (2009) Kant's conception of human dignity. *Kant-Studien* 100(3): 309–331. https://doi.org/10.1515/KANT.2009.018.

Shell SM (2003) Kant on human dignity. In: Kraynak MP and Tinder EG (eds.) *In Defence of Human Dignity: Essays for Our Times.* Indiana: University of Notre Dame Press, pp. 53–80.

Skorpen F, Thorsen AA, Forsberg C and Rehnsfeldt AW (2014) Suffering related to dignity among patients at a psychiatric hospital. *Nursing Ethics* 21(2): 148–162.

Steel Z, Momartin S, Silove D, Coello M, Aroche J and Tay KW (2011) Two year psychosocial and mental health outcomes for refugees subjected to restrictive or supportive immigration policies. *Social Science and Medicine* 72(7): 1149–1156. https://doi.org/10.1016/j.socscimed.2011.02.007.

Stoecker R (2003) Menschenwurde und das Paradox der Entwurdigung. In: R Stoecker (ed.) *Menschenwurde - Annaherung an einen Begriff.* Berlin: Obv and Hpt, pp. 133–151.

Stoecker R (2011) Three crucial turns on the road to an adequate understanding of human dignity. In: Kaufmann P, Kuch H, Neuhauser C and Webster E (eds.) *Humiliation, Degradation, Dehumanization: Human Dignity Violated.* New York: Springer, pp. 7–17.

Sykes G (1958) *The Society of Captives: A Study of a Maximum Security Prison.* 1st ed. New Jersey: Princeton University Press.

Thompson GN and Chochinov HM (2008) Dignity-based approaches in the care of terminally ill patients. *Current Opinion in Supportive and Palliative Care* 2(1): 49–53. https://doi.org/10.1097/SPC.0b013e3282f4cb15.

United Nations (1948) *The Universal Declaration of Human Rights.* New York: United Nations

Van Zyl Smit D and Snacken S (2009) *Principles of European Prison Law and Policy: Penology and Human Rights.* Oxford: Oxford University Press.

Wheeldon J and Faubert J (2009) Framing experience: Concept maps, mind maps and data collection in qualitative research. *International Journal of Qualitative Methods*: 68–83. https://doi.org/10.1177/160940690900800307.

Wilson W (1967) Correlates of avowed happiness. *Psychological Bulletin* 67(4): 294–306. https://doi.org/10.1037/h0024431.

Yates D (2011) *Harry Potter and the Deathly Hallows: Part 2.* California: Warner Bros. Pictures.

2
DETENTION

The existing literature on the experience of men and women in immigration removal centres is bleak, and the findings from my own research do little to dispel this negative image. The women I spoke to in Yarl's Wood felt they were being held captive in a prison. They believed they were being punished, not only unjustly but cruelly. Their treatment, they said, was worse than they would expect for serious and dangerous offenders. Most, if not all, suffered from chronic uncertainty caused by the seemingly arbitrary use of indefinite detention, and the impenetrable pathways to release or removal.

This chapter is informed by interviews of focus groups with 38 women held in detention at the time of interview. The majority of interviews were conducted one to one (18), or involved two women at one time (8), and some involved three or more people at once (11). One interview could be described as a free-flowing focus group, which ranged in size from one interviewee to eight women, on and off, throughout, all discussing the conditions of the centre with me.

Immigration removal centres as prison

All the women I spoke to in Yarl's Wood described this site of administrative detention as a prison. Their belief that they were imprisoned was so strong that when I asked them to explain, many merely laughed. The idea that they might not be in prison was ridiculous. As others have before them (for example, see Bosworth, 2014), they pointed to the building with its gates and the barbed wire. Also, they said, the

DOI: 10.4324/9780367823153-3

actions of staff members and the restrictions placed on their actions and movements within the centre felt penal.

Yarl's Wood opened in 2001 and, like most of the other removal centres in the UK, has the look and feel of a modern prison. Entry to the main units is down a set of stairs from the legal corridor and 'admin block' where centre management, administrative and immigration staff are located. When I was conducting fieldwork, the main site was accessed through a large door at the bottom of a staircase. Outside the main door there was always a collection of people waiting to see immigration or their legal advisors. Women could not access the legal corridor unless a staff member let them through.[1] There was an intercom which they could buzz from their side, but it was difficult to hear what the speaker on the other side was saying. As an example of the closed conditions of the centre at the time, I used this door to access the living areas of Yarl's Wood on route from the admin offices and once came through this door to find two women, one of whom, Micah, was sobbing and yelling into the intercom that she had an appointment earlier, but had missed it. She was distraught and was clutching a brown envelope stuffed with paperwork.[2] The female voice on the other end had little sympathy and was telling Micah she should have turned up on time. I interviewed Micah two weeks later, and she explained that she was very ill with epilepsy and numerous other ailments. She was not feeling well enough to make her legal appointment and after struggling to book an appointment in the first place was terrified that missing the appointment would lead to deportation.

When I asked women what it was about Yarl's Wood that made it feel like a prison, they usually pointed angrily to the barbed wire they could see out the window, or to the large brick walls that surrounded the yards. Samantha had moved to the UK from Jamaica as a young woman on a tourist visa. Her plan was to attend college and make a better life for herself, after suffering from abuse from her own family back home. After her initial visa expired, her grandfather at the time, who also lived in the UK, had promised to help her extend her visa to continue her studies. He died before this could happen, however, and not knowing what to do Samantha continued to live in the UK without a valid visa. Two years before I met her, Samantha had received a prison sentence after an altercation with a former friend. She had spent two years in Downview prison before coming to Yarl's Wood and described to me the similarities between the two institutions:

> The fence that lines it at the back, it is a big fence, when you open your window you look like Downview prison. Because Downview fence is the same. You only can go to the middle of the garden here with walls … it's, if you look it is depressing. Cause it's all building, if you look upside you can see some farm far away, you are like in the middle of nowhere. So the feeling is depressing. Because everywhere you see a door. That's the prison. Door. door. door. door.

As Samantha made clear, the physical similarities between prison and immigration detention affected her mood, making it hard to cope with her confinement. There was a clear link between the appearance of prison and dignity. The high walls, barbed wire, and locked doors were a constant reminder that the Home Office, unfairly, believed women were dangerous to society. Women were unable to escape their confinement, and the environment wore down their mental strength.

Other respondents described similarities between prison and detention regimes. Afiya, who was 23 years old when I interviewed her, had arrived in the UK as an 8-year-old child, brought from Uganda by her parents. She had been in detention for five months when we met, and had served a prison sentence for burglary alongside which she was served a deportation order. She had four children in the UK, aged between 14 and 4. She feared being returned to Uganda. Not only did she remember little about the country, but, as a lesbian, she feared she would be at risk. When I asked Afiya how immigration detention compared to prison, she replied:

> It's the same, but, at least in here you got a bit more freedom to walk around other units. But. It's still locked up at a certain time and queuing for food and them checking up on you all the time and you see officers everywhere. So it is like prison. But only a posher prison.

This view, of Yarl's Wood as a prison, 'but posher', reflects the 'softer' image of immigration detention promoted by removal centres. Women in immigration detention do have access to greater goods and services than those in a women's prison. The women's rooms in Yarl's Wood were, for the most part, twin rooms with a self-contained wet area containing a shower, sink, and toilet. Women were provided with soap to wash, and shampoo in small sachets, though this was decreed inadequate by some women I spoke with, and had free access to razors and sanitary towels.[3]

Women were highly critical of practices which were perceived as especially penal. For most, regular roll counts epitomised the excessive amounts of security they had to endure. Each day women were required to be in their rooms at set points in the day and officers would enter the rooms and count the residents. The counts took place at 7.30 am, 12 pm, 5 pm, and 9.45 pm every day. Luciana had been in detention for one month when I spoke with her. She had a British partner who she had been with for nine years and with whom she had a daughter. Luciana was in the process of a Rule 35 application,[4] which she hoped would allow her release from detention. Her incarceration was causing her considerable extra distress. The lack of control she had in detention triggered feelings of fear resulting from a rape she had suffered in the past. Luciana described how she found the roll count especially upsetting, particularly the manner with which it was conducted:

> You know, they terrible, terrible. In the morning at 7 o'clock in the morning, you know how they come, roll call. OK. You know, we are sleeping and they come like. (Luciana goes out of the room, stomps back in and yells ROLL CALL). Why is this??? You know, we are sleeping, why they have to do that horrible thing. Why don't they say (quietly), roll count, or roll count, normal, or roll count. I don't know why, they have maybe … I don't know.

A number of the women had been victims of domestic violence, sexual assault, or torture at the hands of men. Gendered violence is particularly pertinent in the female asylum system, as conflict-related sexual violence is a clear contributor to the forced migration of this population, and in turn the likelihood of women in detention having suffered from such violence is high (Canning, 2010, 2014, 2017). These experiences had left many fearful of men, and so they were particularly disturbed when male officers entered their room. The policy of the removal centre was that officers would knock before entering rooms. In practice, such knocks were often cursory and followed by an immediate opening of the door whether the officer was welcomed in or not.[5] Women who had no prior experience of imprisonment were also frightened by the implicit threat of roll count. They were concerned they would receive further punishment if they were not able to make it back to their rooms before the count began. While it was unlikely women on their way to their room would receive anything but a firm word from an officer there was an underlying sense that anything could happen in detention and this created a tense atmosphere.

Luciana, who lamented the way in which staff conduct roll count earlier, described how this practice made her feel vilified:

> They really really, they make us feel like we are dangerous people, they feel afraid of us. Look at me! I have never done nothing wrong. I feel as … yes, I don't have papers. But you know, and they made me feel like they lock me, and they make sure I am lock and they look at me like, ok, you have to stay there. Because you … morally … I don't know what they are thinking, but they make me feel really bad.

For Luciana and many others, the constant counting made them feel that staff truly believed they were dangerous. Roll count was incompatible with an establishment which was not intended as a prison, it did little but belittle women and make them feel like 'numbers' and criminals. Her lamentation that she does not know what they are thinking illustrates her inability to find justification in their behaviour, which makes it difficult for women to see the action as anything but morally offensive.

Feeling like a criminal

The physical appearance of Yarl's Wood and its policies made women feel that they were being treated as criminals. Elewa, who was otherwise fairly positive about the conditions of the centre, declared towards the end of our interview how it was the attitude towards her that had the most profound impact on her sense of self:

> Yeah, I think for me, what I really don't like about here, it's the whole attitude. The whole attitude of being treated like immigrations/criminal. That I don't like. Yeah. That is how they make you feel, every single day. Everybody.

Maria, who was originally from South Africa, had spent the four and a half years leading up to her detention living in London. Her husband was British and she had a two-year-old daughter living with family in the community. Like many others in detention, Maria's incarceration had been triggered by missing an appointment at the Home Office. She had reporting requirements as part of an application to remain in the UK, and had missed a scheduled sign-on meeting after taking a week's holiday. The consequence, a period in detention, had taken her by surprise. Although Maria acknowledged that there had been attempts to make her feel comfortable, referring particularly to the hairdressing salon and the library facilities, she was adamant that it still did not feel 'right' to be detained, when she had a home she could go to outside, and because she had committed no criminal offence. The label of criminal profoundly affected Maria's confidence in herself. She was overwhelmed trying to illustrate to anyone who would listen how she was a good person, and was becoming nervous and confused with the effort to maintain the appearance of her notion of someone who was not a criminal.

Some women tried to justify how and why they could be treated as criminals. This attempt to understand was used as a mechanism to cope, as women searched for meaning that would rationalise their treatment. Barbara felt the government warranted the action based on lack of citizenship: 'We are not criminal. But they behave like we are criminal, because we are not British, and that is why.' Barbara felt there was a political agenda behind her treatment by the government as an American, non-citizen. She believed that, as it was an election year (2015), the government were detaining and removing more people to help win votes. This belief helped Barbara maintain her sense of pride; explaining her treatment as a political act was less personal, thus circumventing the offence of not being wanted personally. Samantha used a similar means to defend herself against the perceived attack against her. She argued that her status as an immigrant overcame all other aspects of her identity, and her treatment as 'less than' a UK citizen was the result. Nonetheless Samantha still believed the stripping of all other roles was offensive, and that this practice stripped her of her dignity:

> Me personally yeah, it's like your dignity has been taken away here innit. You ain't got no rights. You're an immigrant and therefore you must have to swallow whatever comes to you. That's not right. We are somebody's children, somebody's mother. Someone's daughter, someone's wife. Someone's sister. A fiancée. Grandmother! We all got them in here yeah. And all we want is treat us like how you want to be treated.

Linked to the stripping of roles, was a sense that all of the identities possessed by women had been eradicated, leaving them with the only justification being that they must be viewed by the Home Office as animals. This conceptual tie between treatment as a criminal and as animal has also been referenced before in detention literature (see Bosworth, 2014; Bosworth and Turnbull, 2015), and is important to the argument that women were not treated with sufficient dignity in detention. Hali had been in immigration detention for 93 days. Originally from Kenya, she was married to a British man. She described her distaste at the treatment of women during transportation to and from the centres especially.[6] 'They say we are animals anyway, so that is why they are doing all that. How can you put a woman in handcuffs that has not committed a crime?' When I asked Barbara if it was possible to have dignified detention, she was clear:

> No. When you house people like cattle in a locked building, with locked doors there is no dignity there. That's meant for people who break the law, and knew they were breaking the law and did it anyway.

Women were not able to justify the criminalised nature of their treatment as morally conceivable. Thus, they believed the Home Office and those working for the institution must believe them to be criminal, and resultantly deserving of harsh treatment, or alternatively, they must be thought of as animals who were unworthy of dignified care. Esther had spent 40 years in the UK, having been brought to the country as a six-year-old. She faced deportation to Ghana after a short prison sentence. She had worked a professional job[7] and would be leaving her three children in their teens and her own mother behind. Her children and other family members had full British citizenship, but Esther told me how she was lax about getting her passport never thinking she would end up in prison and then facing deportation. Esther felt women in detention were animals waiting for slaughter:

> my feeling about this place is … you're like chickens, we're the chickens in, we're the chickens and all they have to do … all we … all we are waiting for is which one they are going to say is to be slaughtered. That's my feeling.

During my time in Yarl's Wood a news story was aired by Channel 4 news, which supported women's views that they were thought of as animals. In undercover footage aired during the programme, staff at the centre are heard to refer to women as '*beasties*' and '*animals*.' Further, guards were heard to suggest violence as a means of dealing with women that would not be considered acceptable for actual animals in captive: 'They're all animals. Caged animals. Take a stick with you and beat them up. Right?' (Channel 4 News, 2015). Most women had watched the programme when it aired. They explained how their worst fears had been realised, as, to perceive treatment as less than human was painful enough, but to have this perception confirmed removed any sense of hope that they were mistaken. The effect on women's sense of self was, as exemplified by Esther, 'devastating.'

Uncertainty

While the UK was still a member of the EU, it was the only enforcement regime in the union that held people in detention indefinitely (HMIP and ICIBI, 2012; Bosworth and Vannier, 2016). Elsewhere in Europe, indefinite detention is considered incompatible with the human rights of liberty and security (de Zayas, 2010). As a result of this indefinite time limit, immigration detention in the UK is characterised by uncertainty (Bosworth, 2014; Griffiths, 2013; Hasselberg, 2016). Men and women often do not know why they have been detained, how long they will be held in detention, nor how to challenge their detention successfully. People in detention commonly describe their inability to know what happens next as a source of anxiety, stress, and a contributor to a host of mental and physical ailments (Hasselberg, 2016).

To be forced into such a state of uncertainty was felt by women in this study as an affront to their sense of dignity. The potentially endless time of detention creates an unusual dynamic experienced by very few other incarcerated populations. The women in this study suffered greatly due to the uncertainty surrounding their time in detention. Those who had never spent time in prison struggled to understand how their ongoing detention could be justified, while former prisoners tried to draw on their experience of imprisonment to make sense of this new form of confinement, but still could not fully understand their new confinement. Women who were mothers were stripped of their identity as carers of children, and unable to justify or explain their detention to their offspring. All women were confused by their detention and were unable to predict what would happen next in their case. All these things caused mental anguish for participants in a situation incompatible with 'dignified' treatment.

The indefinite nature of detention scared women. Even those who had been in detention for relatively short periods of time were anxious, as stories about women who had been in detention for upwards of a year circulated frequently. Luciana told the story of another long-term resident:

> We found one lady is here for 25 months and she go mental. Two three days ago, one week ago I saw her in the church, she was very strong person, incredible. 25 months in this place and at the end, what's happened? She go crazy. She lost her mind. Now she's not well. What is happening??! How can they have one person for two years here? 25 months. 25 months and this lady at the end they go mental. (slaps hands together)

The story of this particularly unwell woman was told to me by several residents and I had seen the person they were referring to walking the hall, clearly unsettled. Another interviewee shared the room next to her, and described how she would often bang on the walls and scream out at night. From all accounts, this woman had been 'just like them' when she first arrived in detention. She had spent time with others socially and appeared no different to any other resident. There were no indications this woman would break down, and as a result, women were anxious this could happen to them too.

Women who were scared for their mental health were not unfounded in their fears. There is well founded evidence, across jurisdictions and disciplines, that immigration detention has a negative effect on the mental health of residents (Engberg, 2013; Kellezi et al., 2019; Kellezi and Bosworth, 2016; McLoughlin and Warin, 2008; Robjant et al., 2009; Steel et al., 2011; Steel and Silove, 2001). In addition, depression, anxiety, and PTSD all become more likely to occur the longer women are held in detention (Bosworth 2016: 303–322, in Shaw, 2016), and individuals' ability to cope with their detention diminishes (Bosworth and Gerlach, 2020).

Indefinite immigration detention made women feel trapped and helpless. Vondra was 70 years old. She was from Jamaica and had severe epilepsy. She had moved to the UK in the early 1990s and explained how her passport and birth certificate had been mislaid. Vondra described to me how she had tried to regularise her visit to the UK early in her stay, and that the Home Office told her they would be in touch to discuss her status. After four years of signing on to the Home Office, Vondra was asked to come in for questioning and was detained from there. I interviewed Vondra alongside a young woman, Afiya, who, with the help of others in the centre, was taking care of Vondra.[8] Vondra had been in detention for five months when we met. She described to me how she felt 'helpless,' 'worthless,' and 'useless' in detention. Every day felt the same to her, and she had nothing to do to increase her sense of self-worth:

> You know, you get up in the morning if you feel to have breakfast or … then lunchtime comes and then you have nothing to do but sit around and look. It's the same story, same attitude, same people, the same everything. Nothing, nothing, absolutely nothing. It's being detained.

Vondra went on to describe how she supposed it could be the same for another 10 years, with the only change that perhaps the staff would decide to be stricter on the residents. Vondra's ruminations here reflect the findings of Griffiths, who described how indefinite time spent incarcerated within a removal centre can feel longer than the lived reality (Griffiths, 2013). Stuck between seemingly indefinite time in detention and the threat of immediate removal women found themselves paralysed, and thus, they showed signs of learned helplessness, such as an apathy about their ability to change their situation, and lack of motivation to keep trying.

Women who had spent time in prison were no less troubled by their indefinite imprisonment. Former prisoners understood their confinement in terms of their stay in prison, and always referenced the differences and similarities between the two institutions. Samantha explained:

> But here … it's really hard. It's hard to cope because when you in a prison, you know you have a day that you is going to be released, but inside of here it is a death sentence. You don't know, you don't know will it be today, tomorrow, the next two years, the next three years. Nobody says anything to you and it's hard doing that. It's hard. It's hard.

Reference to time in detention as a death sentence was not uncommon, as were suggestions that detention was a life sentence. This point further emphasises the vilification felt by women in Yarl's Wood. The only others with similar sentences are prisoners who have committed serious crimes such as murderers, terrorists, or similar. Therefore, women find it hard to feel they are thought of with the same distaste that people feel towards this group of especially immoral offenders.

Former prisoners I spoke with often told me they would prefer to be back in prison amongst the familiarity of the women they had come to know there, the routines they were comfortable with, and serving a determinate sentence. The impact of what they saw as effectively a life sentence destabilised former prisoners. Vicky felt the system was designed to test her. Vicky had served multiple prison sentences, and was comfortable with the function of prison. To her, and to others, prison made sense because a crime was committed, and a sentence served that reflected the harms committed by the individual and then a release day provided to work towards. I asked Vicky what impact indefinite detention had on her, and in her thick South London accent she replied:

> It gives you a headfuck. Excuse me for my word (laughs). It messes your head up. Cause you start thinking, these people are testing me and it's like … do you know how many times I have gone to James[9] and said, please, put me on the first coach back to jail. Because I know my head is straight. Doors are locked, I'm in with my girls. We're doing all time. One day we will get our release innit. What you lot are doing, you lot is giving us a bit of freedom. Doors are opeeen, Associatioooon,[10] but guess what youse lot are just testing, testing, testing.

Some former prisoners felt the government, Home Office, and staff were testing, or pushing them to re-offend or act out while in detention so that this could be used against them when bail or immigration decisions were being made. These women felt vilified by this treatment and were fearful their actions would be misinterpreted and used unfairly against them.

The inability to understand why detention was indefinite also played on the minds of women. Attempts to be freed from detention appeared to be a constant pursuit, but the chances of them being freed from their imprisonment appeared to them down to chance or the ability to pay a substantial fee. Women were fighting against a system that appeared incoherent and inconsistent. This was often compounded by difficulties finding competent lawyers,[11] low levels of education, and sometimes limited English. There are a number of processes people in detention can undertake to try and remain in the UK, and I found as many of the women in this study seemingly trying numerous methods at once, as those who had very little idea what was happening in their case. Luciana summarised the general mood in the centre:

> There are a lot of people don't know what is going to happen. Nobody know. That is the problem, nobody know what is going on. Is no one to come tell us. Oh, look that day you going to have this, or one day you gonna, you have to do this. We have to be looking, oh what I need to send, oh I need to … even sometimes we say we don't know what we are doing but we do it.

Luciana captures here the sometimes-frantic attempts made by people in detention to do anything possible to help their case. Luciana's comment regarding making efforts when the person does not know what it is they are doing was particularly evident in discussions with participants. Women felt there was little sense to the system, and that decisions were made arbitrarily. Afiya, described how this made her feel anxious:

> I find it very scary in here. Because I don't know what to expect. One minute everything is ok, next minute people getting deported for no reason, so I find it, very hard to adjust to … this kind of place, and how the mentality of the people working with you are.

The result of this confusion was a sense of indifference from the government and Home Office towards the residents of the centre. They believed the Home Office did not care what happened to them, and this explained why the system was chaotic; women were not worth the effort required to develop a clear, navigable system of immigration enforcement.

People also described mistakes in the system. Some told me they were not the person the Home Office believed them to be. Anam told me her story through a friend who translated as she spoke very little English herself. Anam told me she was a British citizen, born in the UK but then brought up by her grandmother in Pakistan. When she returned to the UK many years later, she told me the Home Office accused her of holding a fraudulent passport and have since claimed she was a different person. Her ID at the detention centre, she claimed, was in a name that was not hers. Anam's claim appears far-fetched, and such apparent unlawful treatment would be damning to the Home Office, yet, it aligns with the stories of others. Another resident, Vicky, had moved from a European[12] country to the UK as a teenager. She found herself in trouble with the police when she was still very young and had used her cousin's name to avoid trouble. Her cousin was a Somali national, and so, when her deportation order was placed, this historical link was used and a deportation to Somalia attempted. The latter case had been resolved and the Home Office was now attempting to remove Vicky to the European country she was truly from. The difference here, perhaps, is in Vicky's ability to speak English and make concerted efforts to clarify her identity without relying on interpreters or lawyers.

The way in which a judgment is made to detain, release, or remove women was unclear to those affected by these decisions. There was little women could see that linked actions made by themselves or their fellow residents that resulted in a favourable outcome. Women often found the Home Office infuriatingly indifferent to their personal circumstances. Many felt they were not given a chance to explain their actions, or to air their concerns for the well-being of their families to the people making decisions regarding their cases. In many instances, women felt that the Home Office were working against them, picking and choosing which information would work best towards removing them. Ruby was a student who had been taken into detention after the English test she had taken to qualify for her student visa was thought to be fraudulent. She had been in the UK studying for four years before her detention, the interview was conducted in English and Ruby helped me by translating an interview for her roommate also. I asked her what it feels like when the Home Office does not believe your situation:

> It's really painful, to be really honest. That you are trying to convince someone that please, we are not telling that right or wrong. Just give us a chance to prove ourselves. But Home Office not wanting to give a single chance to us. I don't know why they believe in all wrong things, why they not believing all the good things? All the things which are going in our favour they are not going to believe in all these things. And they believe in all the things that are against us, I don't know why.

Ruby illustrates here the impact when an individual is 'grouped' with others, with little regard for individual circumstances. This was especially painful for women in detention, who felt they were grouped with the exceptionally small number of individuals who do try to take advantage of the immigration enforcement and asylum system to remain in the UK. The nature of this grouping led Ruby and others to feel diminished, as though they were not worthy of individual attention or care.

Other women described more personal animus. The Home Office, they believed, simply did not like them, and this was the cause of their troubles. Krista was from Latvia, and had been a victim of trafficking in her country before she came to the UK. She told me how she had used drugs to self-medicate due to her past, using them to numb her emotional trauma, and on becoming addicted turned to shoplifting to support her habit. She had been brought into Yarl's Wood following her prison sentence. Krista had been in detention for 8 months, on multiple occasions she had tried to be released via the bail system with no luck. When I asked her why she thought she was still in detention she replied:

> Stress, angry because some people, I don't know how English system working because some people fight in here get released, some people is a big criminal records and they still get released. And it's affected I don't know, like feel immigration don't like us, I don't know.

Like the other women who formed part of this project, Krista was unable to understand why she was still in detention, nor the way in which she could be released. This was causing her to act out, and along with her roommate she was known as a 'troublemaker' in the centre. This behaviour, however, was explained by Krista as an emotional explosion. She could not cope with her detention and her disruptive actions were one of few ways she could express her feelings. The alternative was to self-harm, and Krista showed me the scars on her arms from this practice while in the centre. She made the point that she had never harmed herself in prison. She was, without doubt, struggling to deal with her time in detention.

Being a mother in detention

Children have not been allowed in Yarl's Wood since 2010. The practice was stopped following extensive campaigning from NGOs, charities, and the Liberal Democratic political party at the time. Immigration detention was deemed too damaging for children (see Medical Justice, 2010), and the practice was stopped with the exceptions reported in the introduction to this book.[13] However, while the detention of children in this centre is now considered unacceptable, parents can now be separated from their young children while their mother, father, or both spend time in immigration detention. This was the case for many women in detention. Luciana, for example, had a young daughter who was born in the UK and had British citizenship through her husband. She described how her continued estrangement from her daughter affected her:

> Imagine, you have your family (laughs) but it make you feel here … you know you didn't steal (starts to cry), you didn't do nothing wrong to no-one. That's what make you feel really bad you know. We have a family, I have a baby. Yesterday she was four years and then, why, are, they have to take too long. Why don't they tell me, why they didn't send me to, why they don't take any decision quickly, you know. They take too long.

Luciana was worried she would have to leave without her daughter, and could not understand why the Home Office was taking so long to make a decision on her case. Samantha had a young boy, aged five, and described to me how she had been maintaining the façade that she was away for work since she had been sentenced to prison. The child was getting older and had started to notice things had changed since Samantha had been in detention. Samantha described what happened when his dad had brought him along to immigration court:

> The other day we take him to the court cause I think, his dad was at the court so he'd have to bring him, take him from school because he would have been late to pick him up. He was screaming, cause he say "mum, I see you on the telly, in that room? What you doing in there, you not coming" and I said, oh bubba, oh I didn't know they wouldn't let me, they shouldn't have said that, but that just came out. Cause I never said nothing at all to him. Cause his perception is that I am at work. So I keep it like that. So I try to buy things for him, to keep it like that. After I said that he was so broken, so I have to be more careful.

Samantha found the distance between her and her son the most difficult part of detention. When she had been in prison, her son was able to visit regularly, he lived in London and she was held in a women's prison that was only a bus ride away from her child's home. Since moving to detention, however, the boy was not able to visit often as his father worked during the week, the cost of visiting was now two rail tickets and the trip would take most of a day. Samantha described vividly the impact this had on her:

> So sometimes I will black, sometimes when the reality hits. I'm here. I'm here from last April … Another time I just blocked it out, can have a laugh with you, because that's me, but it's hurt like hell. My child is out there.

The distance families had to travel limited visits severely, and some mothers explained how their children would need to miss school to visit more regularly. Other mothers described how they discouraged their children to visit so that they would not miss their own weekend activities, sports, or church. Some women also found the visits from their children too hard to cope with, due to the severe heartache caused when visits concluded.

Women felt their roles as mothers were stripped by detention. Krista had three children, daughters aged 17 and 7 and a 10-year-old son. She described to me how her eldest daughter was concerned for the youngest, and Krista described hearing the youngest crying when she called. Her seven-year-old could not understand why her mother had been detained and Krista had been told her daughter waited by the window for her to come home every day. Her children's school were also growing concerned for the children who were regularly in tears. Some mothers were no longer calling their children, because their young children asked questions they were not able to answer about when they were returning home. Both mothers and children found this too upsetting to manage. Immigration detention, and the threat of removal, clearly interrupts the social role formerly maintained by mothers before they were incarcerated. For the women in this study, this reduced their sense of dignity as their identities were diminished and replaced with a sense of failure to perform their role.

Distress and gendered violence

It has been noted elsewhere the disproportionate number of women in immigration detention who have been victims of domestic or gendered violence (Canning, 2014, 2017; Girma et al., 2014). From the interviews conducted for this study, it appears the impact of this for women surfaced in two different frustrations. The first was that detention acted as a trigger for past memories, and the second was that their experience of violence left them unable to enact the gendered roles expected of them for the purpose of their immigration case.

Melia was from Jamaica. She described to me how she had been tortured at home and how this had led to her leaving the country. She had submitted a Rule 35 form to the Home Office, in which she stated a doctor had confirmed she had suffered from torture. Before she was brought into detention, she was receiving treatment for physical and psychological effects of her past experiences in the community. Melia could not rationalise why she was being held in detention and threatened with deportation. Like the women described earlier, she found the immigration rules unfair and arbitrary:

> They haven't even gone through what I have gone through. No hassle and they get their stay, and me? I have to be struggling, I have to be begging, what have I done? Heh? The scars, the wounds. Everything I have. My GP they send me for counselling in London, they treat me. I have gone deaf because of the beating. I do operation because of the beating, and you still refusing me. You know? I am like, wow.

To not be believed, despite clear evidence of her torture, was an offence to Melia's dignity. She felt that her story was being dismissed, and the only explanation for this was that she was in some way considered not trustworthy and that this must be due to being considered of poor character due to her low-status as an 'immigrant' to the UK. Melia was adamant her health was being damaged due to detention, and she suffered from symptoms of PTSD due to her confinement. Afiya had lived in the UK since she was 8 years old had also suffered in the past from gendered violence. She suffered from mental health problems which she found were exacerbated in detention:

> For me, it is very difficult, because sometimes I cry a lot, because I find it brings back memories of things that I've been through that is not nice. Like abuse and … all the emotions of the past just catches up with you, and you find yourself more depressed than ever.

Stories of domestic violence were common during interviews. Participants sometimes described in great detail the violence that their partners had subjected them to. Kim had a substantial scar on her face and described to me how her partner had slashed her when she tried to leave him and told her: 'no-one will ever love me with this scar in me face.' Other participants were in detention after leaving abusive partners who they had come to the UK to marry. Vestine and Elewa, both young women in their early twenties, had both left violent husbands, applied for asylum and were in detention awaiting a decision on their cases. They both explained how they could not go home to their families; Vestine's parents had fled Rwanda and Elewa had kept the breakdown of her marriage secret from her family, fearing it would impact on her mother's safety in Kenya.

Coping in detention

The women who participated in my research while in detention were not coping well. Even those who appeared to be cheerful in the corridors and public areas of the centre would express to me in private considerable distress and suffering caused by their time in detention. They described numerous physical ailments alongside problems with mental health including frequent reference to suicide ideation and self-harm.

Women were undoubtedly stressed by their time in detention and this was leading to loss of memory and general confusion. The stressors of detention, such as how long they would be in detention and if they would finally be removed from the country tired women out mentally. They found they were no longer able to concentrate or remember things like they used to. Maria was suffering from confusion regularly, she tried to explain why she thought this was:

> Yeah, you know when you read a book, or when you are able to … your brain is just going all over the place. You're not able to fire all your brainwaves and think clearly … is it because … oh I … Is it because of all these cameras? Is it that people look at you up front, down. I don't know what it is but you would think more clearly at home, than when you are inside here. You are able here … you just … it's all over the place.

Maria struggled to concentrate on the things she used to enjoy, like reading or writing. She explained how she was forgetting basic spelling.

She described how she, along with a lady from Jamaica, sat for ten minutes as they both tried to remember how to spell 'Jamaica.' They laughed the problem off at the time, but it was still playing on Maria's mind how she, and those around her, struggled to complete tasks that would seem simple in their own homes.

Vee, who was originally from Granada, explained how she felt her memory was fading in Yarl's Wood. Vee had been in detention for 11 months at the time we met, she had served a prison sentence before this and lamented how her memory in prison was strong. She had been writing a book when she arrived in detention, but had recently 'given up.' She described how she had begun writing notes to herself because she would wander to the shop and forget why she had needed to go there in the first place:

> If I have to go to the shop and I will remember what I have to, because I leave my room to go to the shop, not a few minutes ago for this tin of milk, but I forget. I forget the key in healthcare I have to go back for the keys.

This memory loss scared Vee, she was only 30 years old and fearful that she would remain forgetful in the future. For Vee the loss of memory was linked to an inability to cope with the indefinite nature of her detention, which she referred to as a death sentence. Vee described how she had been in detention so long, her emotions were becoming internalised, and this was also terrifying for her:

> When I feel so low inside tear don't come out anymore. These tears dropped inside of me and that is really bad when I start crying inside. So sometimes I try my best to see the tears would come out, but the tears still not come out. It's hard for your tears to come out. And the tears are falling inside me. It's really bad. Cause it, what can I get, my memory and at my age I don't want to have memory loss. But I have to keep on asking, I write it down so I know when I come back, I will put down the key and I will search everywhere and the key is right there. It's really hard. It's hard, it is frustrating.

Vee's experience here shows how her sense of self was severely affected by detention. She felt she could no longer trust her own memory, and with this began to second guess who she was as a person. Consequently, her self-esteem and sense of self-worth were substantially reduced.

Women described to me many existing physical medical conditions including diabetes, heart problems, asthma, arthritis, stomach ulcers, and epilepsy. Most of the conditions were pre-existing, though most participants were clear that their time in detention had either exacerbated their condition or that they were not getting the treatment that they required. Other women described undiagnosed symptoms such as excessive vaginal bleeding or blood in their stool along with headaches and difficulties sleeping. These women equally felt they were not getting the care they required.

Vee, alongside her memory problems, was also suffering from multiple health issues. She was suffering from stomach pain and trying to have an ultrasound organised. She was on medication for a sore stomach and high blood pressure, and she told me they had put her on something for her mind since she was in detention 'because I'm mental.' She explained to me the struggles she had getting treatment from healthcare and how they exacerbated her problems. She felt healthcare did not believe her, and that the staff were uncaring and rude to her. She described to me her attempt to take back control of her health, but how it had backfired:

> One time I tell them I'm going to go to the room, the tablets that I've got in the room I will take them all and lie down and die with my pride and dignity because here, it is not even for a dog to come. That's when they took away my medication from me. Because I reached to that, that there was no other help but just to die.

Much to Vee's upset, her use of agency in this example had a detrimental effect on her ongoing experience of detention, as, after her threats to her own life, healthcare no longer allowed her to have medication in her own room. Instead, she had to visit healthcare for each pill. She felt infantilised by this practice, that she was less than able to manage her own health as an adult woman.

Depression, anxiety, and stress were common for interviewees in detention. The women I spoke with were open about these feelings and many explained how they were on medication for their conditions, or should be on medication but were having trouble accessing what they needed. Women employed a number of coping mechanisms to help them remain positive; however, these actions were limited by the restrictiveness of their confinement, poor access to mental health support, and the indefinite nature of their detention. The resulting effect was a population in severe distress, self-harm, and suicide ideation.

Micah, whom I first met at the door to legal visits, detailed how her physical health had deteriorated in detention because of the stress of her situation. Micah was only 19 and appeared even younger due to her diminutive size. She had come to the UK from Kazakhstan on a valid visa and had been detained after turning to the Home Office for help when the family member who was supporting her in the UK told her she could no longer stay with him. Micah eventually lost eight kilograms in the five months she had spent in detention. She was unable to stomach most of the food in Yarl's Wood and, after reaching the stage where she was unable to eat most things without vomiting, she resorted to only eating pot-noodles from the shop. Micha's epilepsy was also becoming worse and she was suffering from fits and blackouts regularly. She told me how she thought she was losing her mind, and was unable to think from stress. When I spoke with Micah, she had spent three months in detention, she was released after five months. I met her again in the community some months later, and continue her story in the following chapter.

Micah's story is a more extreme example of how mental health can be affected by stress and deteriorating physical health. The stress she experienced, however, was not unfamiliar to the women who participated in the research. Women lamented the impact of the stress of detention had on their mental health. Vee explained how she had, at first, used her friends to help relieve her stress, but after 11 months she was no longer able to find comfort from them. She had begun to withdraw from everyone:

> There is no happiness … I used to go to Dove,[14] sit down, chat with, sit outside in the garden. I just don't want to go nowhere. What I do, I pull the curtain, I close the door, lock the door behind me and I lie down.

Vee was not alone in this technique of withdrawal. For her, it was all she felt she could to do cope, and this was echoed by others who preferred the relative serenity of their room to the generalised distress that characterised the atmosphere of Yarl's Wood. The distress of others had a severe impact on women, who, even if their own mood was relatively high, felt themselves grow more concerned as they witnessed others change from 'normal' to distressed and sometimes, as in the case described earlier, to become mentally unstable. The indefinite and arbitrary nature of their detention made them feel the same could happen to them at any time.

Some women shared with me candid stories of distress, self-harm, and suicide ideation and attempts. Dana was the roommate of Krista, and had a similar backstory of trafficking and drug dependence. She had been trafficked in Latvia at the age of 13, and, though she had been able to get away from her traffickers and come to the UK, she had taken hard drugs to help her cope. She had received a prison sentence for shoplifting and this is how she found herself in immigration detention and facing removal from the country. Dana explained how she was charged with the assault of an officer in detention, which she suggested was unintentional. After learning of her charge in court she had decided it was too much. She described to me, in detail, what happened next:

> After I don't want to leave, I put ligature around my neck, the officer come they were so shocked because I was so red and if maybe couple minutes I will die. I never self-harm in my life, I start to self-harm in here.

I asked Dana and Krista what it was, that made them turn to self-harm in detention, when they had previously not done so before. For Dana, it was the indefiniteness of her imprisonment: 'We feel this if for life, we feel we never go out from this place.' Krista added that detention felt like a double punishment to her, she had already been punished and served her time in prison and could not fathom why they were being penalised further: 'And like human rights, not to be punished twice you know and we still get punished and punished and punished. Whatever we ask, no no no no. It's very stressful, really angry, upset.'

Conclusion

Painted here is a bleak portrait of women's lives in immigration detention, and one that illustrates how women do not feel they are treated with dignity in this space. Residents repeatedly described situations in which they lacked autonomy and were made to feel dependent and infantilised (see also Bosworth and Turnbull, 2015; Canning, 2017). The 'pain' of autonomy is well documented in Sykes (1958) classic pains of imprisonment text. In Sykes's work, the childlike state caused by a lack of autonomy is dangerous to the health of the prisoner. Likewise, in the dignity of patients was seen to be threatened in health care when patients are treated as though they were children (Gallagher and Seedhouse, 2002). For women in detention, the lack of autonomy while contained was fundamental to their experience.

In addition, women felt the appearance of Yarl's Wood was akin to a prison, and that their indefinite detention was representative of the government and Home Office believing them to be as morally defunct as the UK's 'worst' criminals. The women are not alone in this perception of criminality. Even the officers in charge of their care confessed to Bosworth and Turnbull (2015) that the carceral environment of immigration removal centres led them to believe that there 'must' be some justification for why the people in their care were being deprived of their liberty that suggested they were in some way dangerous. Women felt this, and felt vilified and shamed by their criminalisation and suffered greatly from a loss of self-esteem as a result (see also Bosworth, 2017; Bosworth and Kellezi, 2012; Griffiths, 2012; Silverman and Massa, 2012).

Gendered experiences of detention were also found in the stories of women. Mothers were unable to fulfil their roles as carers and felt this identity had been stripped from them, causing substantial distress. Not only did this impact on women, but there was substantial evidence that their children were suffering the secondary effects of their parents' detention, including the stigma and shame felt by having their mother 'in prison.' This finding mirrors the impact of imprisoned mothers by Minson (2018) when she analysed the harms of maternal imprisonment. Women who had previously suffered from gendered violence were especially vulnerable to all the violations described to dignity here (see also Canning, 2014, 2017), and yet this population make up a substantial portion of women interviewed for this project.

Not surprisingly then, mental and physical health problems were prolific in the centre. Women suffered from extreme stress, anxiety, depression, PTSD, and a host of physical problems exacerbated by these conditions. Women were not coping well with their confinement, and this could be evidenced by the number of women describing to me both idealised and real attempts at self-harm or suicide. It was evidentially clear that dignity was lacking in immigration detention.

Notes

1 This door has since been unlocked, allowing women access to the legal corridor without the need to be buzzed through.

2 The brown envelope containing paperwork is common in removal centres, and is one of the defining characterises of these spaces. Men and women tend to tote them around, keeping them safe for when they need the contents to defend their case.
3 These items were kept in wing offices. Sanitary towels were kept on a shelf in the corner and women were able to collect them when required. Razors were available on request from an officer in the office, and had to be returned after use. Offices were staffed by male and female staff.
4 The process of release from detention based on evidence of torture.
5 The problem of officers entering after cursory knocks has been identified in both official reviews (Lampard, 2016) and inspections (HMIP, 2015) of Yarl's Wood Removal Centre. I also witnessed this behaviour while interviewing women in their bedrooms.
6 Hali was referring to any instance where women are taken to and from the centre, this can be a transfer from a police station, visits to hospital, or trips to the airport when attempts at removal have been made.
7 Esther never mentioned what this job entailed, just that it was a good job in an office.
8 It was evident to me that Vondra needed this unofficial assistance from other residents, as, throughout the interview, she nodded off to sleep regularly.
9 The names of staff have also been changed to protect anonymity.
10 Notably, the term 'association' is from prison institutions, meaning the free time prisoners have outside of education and work.
11 Difficulties in finding and keeping competent lawyers from detention has also been heavily criticised in official reports (Coussey, 2014; HMIP, 2015; HMIP and ICIBI, 2012; Lampard, 2016), by NGOs (BID, 2005; Girma et al., 2015; Phelps, 2009) and in academic writing (Bosworth, 2011b, 2014; Gill, 2009a).
12 Vicky's country of origin has been removed to protect her anonymity.
13 Families with children should not be held in immigration removal centres; however, they can be held in 'pre-departure accommodation' for 72 hours. However, Ministerial review can be sought for an extended stay of up to a week (McGuiness and Gower, 2017).
14 Dove is one of the two main residential wings at Yarl's Wood.

References

BID (2005) *Fit to Be Detained? Challenging the Detention of Asylum Seekers and Migrant with Health Needs*. London: Bail for Immigration Detainees

Bosworth M (2011) Human rights and immigration detention in the United Kingdom. In: Dembour M-B and Kelly T (eds.) *Are Human Rights for Migrants? Critical Reflections on the Status of Irregular Migrants in Europe and the United States*. Abingdon: Routledge, pp. 165–183.

Bosworth M (2014) *Inside Immigration Detention*. Oxford: Oxford University Press.

Bosworth M (2017) Immigration detention and penal power: A criminological perspective. In: Flynn MJ and Flynn MB (eds.) *Challenging Immigration Detention—Academics, Activists, Policymakers*. London: Edward Elgar, pp. 52–65.

Bosworth M and Gerlach A (2020) Quality of life in detention results from MQLD questionnaire data collected in Gatwick IRC (Brook House and Tinsley House), Heathrow IRC (ColnBrook and Harmondsworth), Yarl's Wood IRC. Morton Hall IRC, and Dungavel IRC: July 4–September 20, 2019. Oxford. Available at: https://www.law.ox.ac.uk/sites/files/oxlaw/mqld_2019_report_for_publication_16.03.20.pdf.

Bosworth M and Kellezi B (2012) Quality of Life in Detention: Results for MQLD Questionnaire Data Collected in IRC Yarl's Wood, IRC Tinsley House, and IRC Brook House, August 2010 - Hune 2011. (February).

Bosworth M and Turnbull S (2015) Immigration detention and the expansion of penal power in the UK. In: Reiter K and Koenig A (eds.) *Extreme Punishment*. London: Palgrave, pp. 50–67.

Bosworth M and Vannier M (2016). Comparing immigration detention in Britain and France: A matter of time? *European Journal of Migration and Law* 18(2): 157–176. https://doi.org/10.1163/15718166-12342097

Canning V (2010) Who's human? Developing sociological understandings of the rights of women raped in conflict. *International Journal of Human Rights* 14(6): 849–864. https://doi.org/10.1080/13642987.2010.512127.

Canning V (2014) Women, asylum and the harms of detention. *Criminal Justice Matters* 98(1): 10–11.

Canning V (2017) *Gendered Harm and Structural Violence in the British Asylum System*. Abingdon: Routledge. https://doi.org/10.4324/9781315720975.

Channel 4 News (2015) *Yarl's Wood: Undercover in the Secretive Immigration Centre*. Channel 4. Available at: https://www.channel4.com/news/yarls-wood-immigration-removal-detention-centre-investigation.

Coussey M (2014) *Yarl's Wood Independent Monitoring Board Annual Report 2014*, pp. 1–25. Available at: http://www.imb.org.uk/wp-content/uploads/2015/06/Yarls-Wood-IRC-2014.pdf.

de Zayas A (2005) Human rights and indefinite detention. *International Review of the Red Cross* 87(857): 15. https://doi.org/10.1017/S1816383100181172.

Engberg M (2013) The impact of immigration detention on the mental health of torture survivors is poorly documented–A systematic review. *Danish Medical Journal* 60(11): A4728. DOI: 10.1016/S0924-9338(13)76202-3.

Gallagher A and Seedhouse D (2002) Dignity in care: The views of patients and relatives. *Nursing Times* 98(43): 38–41.

Gill N (2009) Governmental mobility: The power effects of the movement of detained asylum seekers around Britain's detention estate. *Political Geography* 28(3): 186–196. https://doi.org/10.1016/j.polgeo.2009.05.003.

Girma M, Radice S, Tsangarides N, et al. (2014) *Detained: Women Asylum Seekers Locked up in the UK*, pp. 1–48. London: Women for Refugee Women.

Girma M, Kershaw I, Lousley G, et al. (2015) *I Am Human: Refugee Women's Experiences of Detention in the UK*. London: Women for Refugee Women.

Griffiths M (2012) Anonymous aliens? Questions of identification in the detention and deportation of failed asylum seekers. *Population, Space and Place* 18(6): 715–727. https://doi.org/10.1002/psp.1723.

Griffiths M (2013) Living with uncertainty: Indefinite immigration detention. *Journal of Legal Anthropology* 1(3): 263–286. https://doi.org/10.4059/jla.2013.2616.

Hasselberg I (2016) *Enduring Uncertainty: Deportation, Punishment and Everyday Life*. Oxford: Berghahn.

HMIP (2015) *Report of an Unannounced Inspection of Yarl's Wood Immigration Removal Centre*. London:HM Inspectorate of Prisons

HMIP and ICIBI (2012) *The Effectiveness and Impact of Immigration Detention Casework*. London:HM Inspectorate of Prisons.

Kellezi B and Bosworth M (2016) Mental health, suicidal thoughts and self-harm Inside immigration detention. *SSRN Electronic Journal* (November): 1–7. https://doi.org/10.2139/ssrn.2867358.

Kellezi B, Bowe M, Wakefield JRH, McNamara N and Bosworth M (2019) Understanding and coping with immigration detention: Social identity as cure and curse. *European Journal of Social Psychology* 49(2): 333–351. https://doi.org/10.1002/ejsp.2543.

Lampard K (2016) *Independent Investigation into Concerns about Yarl's Wood Immigration Removal Centre*. (January). London: SERCO.

McGuiness T and Gower M (2017) *Immigration Detention in the UK: An Overview*. Briefing Paper Number 7294. London: House of Commons.

McLoughlin P and Warin M (2008) Corrosive places, inhuman spaces: Mental health in Australian immigration detention. *Health and Place* 14(2): 254–264. https://doi.org/10.1016/j.healthplace.2007.06.008.

Medical Justice (2010). *State Sponsored Cruelty - Children in Immigration Detention*. London. Available at: http://www.crin.org/docs/Medical_justice.pdf.

Minson S (2018) Direct harms and social consequences: An analysis of the impact of maternal imprisonment on dependent children in England and Wales. *Criminology and Criminal Justice*: 1–18. https://doi.org/10.1177/1748895818794790.

Phelps J (2009) *Detained Lives: The Real Cost of Indefinite Immigration Detention*. (January).London: Detention Action.

Robjant K, Hassan R and Katona C (2009) Mental health implications of detaining asylum seekers: Systematic review. *The British Journal of Psychiatry* 194(4): 306–312. https://doi.org/10.1192/bjp.bp.108.053223.

Shaw S (2016) *Review into the Welfare in Detention of Vulnerable Persons: A Report to the Home Office by Stephen Shaw*. London: HMSO, CM9186.

Silverman SJ and Massa E (2012) Why immigration detention is unique. *Population, Space and Place* 18(6): 677–686. https://doi.org/10.1002/psp.1720.

Steel Z and Silove DM (2001) The mental health implications of detaining asylum seekers. *The Medical Journal of Australia* 175(11–12): 596–599.

Steel Z, Momartin S, Silove D, et al. (2011) Two year psychosocial and mental health outcomes for refugees subjected to restrictive or supportive immigration policies. *Social Science and Medicine* 72(7): 1149–1156. https://doi.org/10.1016/j.socscimed.2011.02.007.

Sykes G (1958) *The Society of Captives: A Study of a Maximum Security Prison*. 1st ed. Princeton, NJ: Princeton University Press.

3

RELEASE

From my time conducting fieldwork in detention, I knew that being released from these institutions was a source of joy. In Yarl's Wood, women often celebrated the release of others by cheering loudly and singing. On their way out, people said their goodbyes to friends they had made in detention, often moving with some difficulty towards the reception area through the crowd of women that formed around them. It was with some sorrow, then, that I discovered in the second stage of this project that women's lives post-detention were still grim.

Over a 6-month period, I spoke with 12 women who had spent time in immigration detention. Some women had been in detention for only 11 days, others had been there for up to 7 months. All of them were struggling with their life post-detention. Women experienced their new lives in the community as another form of incarceration, and their 'freedom' was paradoxical. While they had been freed from the bars and razor wire of the removal centre, their lives were heavily restricted by reporting conditions, they felt socially excluded, and lived in constant fear of re-detention. Some women were left powerless by inadequate housing arrangements and conditions and were left vulnerable to further abuses of power from both the state and individuals they relied upon to survive.

What happens after detention?

An individual who has been released from immigration detention, but who has not been granted the right to remain, is not legally allowed

DOI: 10.4324/9780367823153-4

to work in paid employment. The women in this project relied on the government, charities, and/or their friends or partners to survive. Those who were waiting on decisions for an asylum claim, but had yet to receive a decision from the Home Office, were provided with support from the government. This typically involved some type of accommodation and provision of food. Women described several ways of sustenance were provided to them, from collecting an allowance from the post office, to having the use of a card-based system which they could spend in select stores. Alternatively, some people were provided with food at their accommodation and received no income source for their nourishment needs.

Women who had received a negative decision from the Home Office on an asylum claim, or who had been released pending a decision related to another type of claim to stay,[1] were not provided with any assistance from the government. This group of women, without state support, were dependent on charities, families, and friends for housing and all other means for survival. It was not always clear, to the women, or to me, what they were entitled to, or at which point of their immigration enforcement process exactly they were, or were not, supported by the government. In reality, they were often dependent on different sources for survival. The level of support also appeared to vary, and women were not always willing to declare the details of their financial situation. But in any case, women were limited due to their inability to earn a living through employment.

All the women I spoke to wanted to work and provide for themselves. Financial independence, they said, would not just assist them with practical matters, but was central to their sense of self. Unable to work, many struggled. Dana, who was from Oman, had spent a month in detention. As a lesbian she felt unable to return to her country of birth where she would be at risk. Dana had been detained in three different institutions, starting in Dungavel IRC before moving on to Colnbrook IRC's women's unit and then finally Yarl's Wood IRC before she was released. When we spoke, Dana had been out of detention for approximately a year. She was not receiving funding from the government, although she had been trying to organise accommodation through the National Asylum Support Service (NASS) who house people seeking asylum through government contract. She was surviving on handouts from friends. She had made a friend online who would send her money, and she was living with her ex-partner. Dana found this dependence unpleasant. It undermined her self-confidence and her sense of self. 'Living off other people,' as she put it, made her 'hate myself.' In a rare positive account of her time in detention, Dana said that she had been happy that she could work there, earning around £15 a week working in the kitchen. Dana found the inability to work degrading. For her, working and providing for herself offered the greatest defence against losing her sense of self:

> I don't brush everyone with the same brush, but I think with me because with me, allow me to keep my pride, my dignity, my self-respect, self-worth everything like this, let me go do my own job, do whatever you want to do guys, but let me do my own job. Earn my own living, build my own life.

The state of dependence experienced here by Dana was a common theme throughout the interviews and easily the most common grievance raised by women in the community. Brenda was seeking asylum, she had fled her home village in Uganda after her husband was murdered in front of her and their children. She approached a man for help in her own country, who promised to send her to safety in the UK. Instead, she said, he trafficked her into the sex trade. She escaped, and began a life in England using the identity of another woman. After some years, she was caught by immigration officers when they came to her shared accommodation in search of someone she lived with. He was not at home, but the passport Brenda had been using was flagged as wanted by the Home Office and so she was taken to immigration detention. She was released one month and one week later after applying for asylum, approximately five years before her interview with me. She told me she was not aware of the concept of asylum before she was detained.

Despite being trafficked, when she was released from Yarl's Wood, Brenda was not initially offered financial assistance from the British government. Unable to pay her rent, she was soon evicted from her apartment. She stayed with friends when she could, but often took to sleeping on buses in London. Brenda would board a bus at 7 pm at night and ride until the morning when she would go to a friend's place for a shower before spending the day on the streets. When interviewed, she had been provided with NASS housing, but was still surviving on £30 cash a week which she received from what she referred to as social services. She described how her limited means impacted on her sense of humanity:

> It is really hard, hard thing to do. When you are just there. Without working, you want to eat, sleep, want to dress, do the things like human beings … you can't … I feel sometimes so bad, if I have to go to my friend, please can you give me five pounds, I want to buy this, you feel that sometimes now most of them, sometimes they get fed up. I don't bother them.

As Brenda's words make it clear, her experiences in the community undermined her sense of autonomy and independence. Such matters are closely linked to 'feeling human' in academic literature pertaining to health and social care (Madan, 1992; Miller and Keys, 2001a; Moore and Miller, 1999; Sautier, Vehling, and Mehnert, 2014), prisons (Liebling, 2004; Liebling and Maruna, 2005; Singer, 1972) and in existing works on immigration detention (Griffiths, 2013; Turnbull, 2016) and with people seeking asylum in the community (Canning, 2010, 2017; Hasselberg, 2016).

Where Brenda was reliant on charity for her living, others depended on their partners. This arrangement, while preferable, was not without its problems. Women worried about their lack of independence. Larissa, who was from Kurdistan, had been studying accountancy in the UK before her detention. She had applied for an extension to her student visa, but this had been declined by the Home Office. She appealed the decision, and while awaiting a decision, married her partner, who was a European citizen. The Home Office believed the wedding was fraudulent and sent immigration officers to her wedding party to detain her. She spent three months in detention. When we spoke, Larissa had been released for five months. Although happy to be out of Yarl's Wood, she was frustrated by the employment restrictions which left her unable to work as a cleaner alongside her studies as she had been prior to detention. Her unemployment, she felt, made her a burden on her husband and on the tax payers of Britain. She had written to the Home Office to request that she could continue to work but had not received a response.

Women simply could not understand the restrictions on paid employment. Ryane had been trafficked from Nigeria and caught by immigration when she was working as a prostitute to repay her 'debt' to the woman who brought her to the UK. She had spent six weeks in detention during her latest visit but had been detained three times since she first arrived in the country in 2011. She found the restriction on work to be dehumanising. She was worth less than an animal in Britain. Pets were treated with more care than she had been, she insisted. Other countries, she also insisted, allowed people seeking asylum to work and pay their bills while waiting for their papers. Ryane did not believe her friends back home would believe the way she was treated in the UK:

> Sometimes if I told my friends other country, look what is going on like, that kind of thing doesn't exist! I say yes it exist here! Because the way that they are saying on the TV is not the way they are doing.

Like the women I spoke with in Yarl's Wood, Ryane believed that Britain presented a false image to the rest of the world. Despite its claims to be a country of rights, in a familiar refrain, Ryane believed her human rights had been denied. Her sense of having been 'tricked' into believing the UK was a safe haven added an additional layer to her feelings of injustice at the hands of the Home Office. As with others in the study, Ryane believed she would not be in the UK and in their present, difficult situation had she known the hostile environment in which she would find herself. In her account, the relationship between self-realisation and dignity, and how easily it is undermined, was clear.

Women who were supported by the government, at first glance, appeared to have greater financial security than those who were not. They at least had some kind of income. These women were provided with accommodation and a debit card with which they were able to purchase goods from approved stores. Yet, they all were unhappy. The 'Azure' cards, in particular, were cited as a great source of frustration and embarrassment. Azure cards look like debit cards, but they can only be used at certain stores such as Tesco, Sainsbury's, Boots, and Mothercare. Most importantly, they cannot be used to withdraw cash or to purchase bus passes or rail tickets. At the time of my research, single women received £36 a week on their Azure card, while mothers with children could receive up to £80. At the end of each week the card was reset. Any unused funds were wiped so that women were never able to save for bigger purchases.

Azure cards are often mentioned in research with men and women seeking asylum in the community (Allsopp et al., 2014). The use of the cards and other similar voucher systems has been heavily criticised for restricting the autonomy of people seeking asylum in existing work (British Red Cross and Boaz Trust, 2013; Doyle, 2009; Hamilton and

Harris, 2009; Mulvey, 2009; Phillimore et al., 2010). They have also been shown to cause users to feel ashamed and stigmatised (Klein and Williams, 2012; Refugee Action, 2006). The women in this study experienced many of these feelings.

The women in this study were not unaware of the current political climate in the UK where migrants and people seeking asylum have so often been vilified by popular press as burdens on the state (see Canning, 2017; Fekete, 2001). Azure cards highlighted their dependence on the government to the public. Many found them embarrassing to use. ‘It’s not easy to live on that, Azure card,’ Ryane exampled,

> it’s not easy because it is something that, you understand, is hell like because you don’t have financial because it is just particular place that you need to buy something. Sometimes it is shameful to bring that kind of card, because some people are like, what is this? Even in front of a queue of people, they was like, what is this?

Shopping assistants unfamiliar with Azure cards could be particularly insensitive. Ryane, and others, described shopping assistants holding up the checkout lines while they waited for managers to come confirm the cards were authentic. Their questions drew attention to the women’s status as people seeking asylum, rendering it their most important quality, thereby denying the rest of their identity.

The additional funds provided for children was also restrictive. Julie was from The Democratic Republic of Congo, she had a ten-month-old baby at the time of interview. She was pregnant with her child when she was in detention for a month in 2014. Julie lived in shared NASS accommodation and was provided with an Azure card containing £80 of credit each week. She was pleased to have the support of an income, but found the choice of shops restrictive. She explained how Mothercare, which was the only shop where she could buy things for her baby, was expensive. She told me how clothes for the baby cost up to £50, which meant she had nothing left to buy clothes for herself. She similarly found entertaining her small child difficult without funds for toys or activities; her accommodation lacked even the most basic of entertainment such as a television or radio.

Other women observed they could purchase food and goods for a much cheaper price at local markets if they had cash. Similarly, culturally specific items were often not available in mainstream stores, and women would rather shop at local nation-based food stores. Those who had allowances provided through the post office or from charities were at least able to choose where to spend their money, though they still found it difficult to budget on £36 a week.

Women were creative in their management of Azure cards, finding ways to work within the system to make their lives better. A number had friends who would buy their own groceries with their Azure card, and give women the cash so that they could buy goods from their own choice of retailer. Some, however, did not know anyone who could help them exchange their credit for cash, or were too embarrassed to ask repeatedly for help. Phoebe, who was from Kenya and had been given right to remain in the UK had two young children, aged around seven and two. She had been pregnant with her elder daughter when she was detained for three months. Phoebe was provided with an Azure card to purchase goods for her herself and her daughter once she was born. To get around the restrictions of the card, Phoebe would wait outside her local Tesco each week and approach shoppers to ask if they could help. Her success in gaining help was variable, she was often yelled at by people who thought she was doing something illegal, while others spent £36 but returned her less than this amount, knowing there was little she could do about it. Phoebe felt ashamed to be waiting outside the shop each week and was eventually banned from the Tesco when a security guard noticed her spending time near the store regularly. She described how she was further shamed when the guard shouted at her and told her to go away.

In addition to restrictions on food and goods purchases, women were also unable to purchase bus or train tickets with the Azure cards. If they were to travel further than walking distance, they required an additional source of funding for the trip. Ryane explained how she was unable to visit friends as she lived far from Birmingham City Centre. She felt that she was stuck in her house, and was only able to attend support groups if they were able to help her to buy a bus ticket. She lived with three others in her house, but explained that her housemates were unable to speak English and so she was unable to communicate with them. She described a miserable existence where she often stayed in her room during the day, crying and upset.

The restrictions placed on women that stopped them from seeking employment felt unfair and deliberately punitive. The resulting dependence on families, friends, charities, or the government was hard to bear. Women struggled to comprehend why the Home Office would stop them from being functioning members of society when they were all motivated to work and build a life for themselves in the UK. Their treatment left them feeling unwanted, frustrated and resentful of their position in what felt like an underclass of the population. Renas, who had been an academic in her home country, was seeking asylum due to conflicts with her work on human rights and the government in her country of birth. She was regularly offered academic work but was unable to accept for fear the Home Office would find out and use this against her application for asylum. Renas was clear that restricting her ability to work was an offence to her sense of dignity, as she explains here:

> Actually, Home Office and Immigration they take our dignity completely they took it. This against human rights. The best thing for every man in the world has dignity. You work, and you want to get money, you get clothes, you eat, for what? To keep your dignity. But if the Home Office treat you like this way, and they attack and they fight your dignity it is more hard than they give you to injury in an indirect way.

Renas, along with others, felt the restrictions were deliberately designed to make their lives hard, and thus encourage them to leave the country. Women felt the government did not believe their stories. Only Phoebe, who had been waited for six years post-detention to obtain lawful immigration status as a refugee in the UK, was allowed to work. Her pleasure in this basic right was immense: 'So yeah, I am happy cause you know, I can see the future. I am happy now, the way I am living I am just happy. I feel happy, I feel now I can see the future of my children.'

The implications of exclusion through restriction and deprivation were devastating for women. As described by others, the 'othering' and exclusion of women from society is damaging to their mental and physical health (Allsopp et al., 2014; Canning, 2017; Hamilton and Harris, 2009; Mulvey, 2009; Phillimore et al., 2010; Refugee Action, 2006). For women who had spent time in detention, their lack of autonomy to earn an income and thus direct their own lives felt like continued incarceration and exacerbated the feelings of vilification they experienced in removal centres.

Women who were supported by the Home Office while their asylum case was ongoing were provided with accommodation. For the women interviewed for this project, the government assisted accommodation ranged from a bed in a hostel to a room in a share house. Women who were not provided with support from the government were either living with their partner, or had found accommodation through the help of a charity.

Hostels were uniformly described in negative terms. Women found them restrictive, unclean, and noisy. Participants were provided with food in these establishments, but complained that the quality of the meals was poor and the meal times limiting. Amra had moved to the UK to study, but then claimed asylum later after her family situation deteriorated at home and her life was threatened. She had been detained for 11 days after her asylum interview. On release, Amra was sent to a hostel. She described to me how the food arrangements there rendered her community-based accommodation merely an extension of her detention:

> They provide breakfast early in the morning, 7-30 and after that in between 12 and 2 they provide lunch and 5 o clock to 7 o clock they provide dinner. So it is similar to detention, actually no difference.

Hostels also had restrictive reporting measures that bore at least a passing resemblance to the heavily criticised roll count used in detention. Women were required to leave their bedrooms and sign-in at reception at various times during the day, including early in the morning. Renas explained how difficult this was for her due to the medication she was taking for depression at the time:

> It is like a prison, because if you go out from hostel, you have to sign and every morning you have to sign. Every morning. And at that time I was taking my depression, it make me sleepy in the morning, I can't sleep in the night, in the morning I fall asleep. I say to them I can't, I am sleepy in the morning, at 7, at 8 they ask me to do sign.

The restrictive food regimes and reporting measures of these hostels were an unwelcome reminder of women's time in detention. The feeling of vilification, suspicion, and lack of trust developed in removal centres was reinforced by the experiences in hostels. Though technically 'free,' women felt no less vilified by their new environments than they had in detention.

Women in shared houses were not restricted in their movements, but, as they had been in Yarl's Wood, they were still unable to choose with whom they lived. Brenda did not enjoy living with her housemates. One man, who would regularly become angry and kick doors, was particularly difficult. Echoing the words of those in detention, Brenda described her living accommodation as a form of mental torture. She was unable to find peace in her home and had no funds to go elsewhere when she needed a calm space to deal with her depression. Other women were victims of bullying in their homes and told me how their housemates were openly hostile towards them.

Still more similarities existed between the accommodation provided by the Home Office and immigration detention. Like people in detention, women in Home Office accommodation were moved regularly between houses and could be asked to leave at short notice if they received a negative outcome for their case. Renas explained how she felt that as soon as she would begin to make friends and start to get to know the local services in her new city she would be moved again. She was never provided with a reason for the moves, and had no choice but to go where she was sent. Renas considered this to be harassment: 'is kind of attack to us. Is this right? Is there respect human right to do this with us? To move us? From many cities, many places.' The distress felt by women when they were moved, and before, with the constant threat of relocation, reflects again the extension of practices experienced by women in immigration detention. Both Gill (2009) and Griffiths (2014) describe how the uncertainty surrounding the movement of people throughout the detention estate resulted in feelings of depersonalisation and instability. Gill particularly suggests this practice helps to reinforce the idea that people in immigration removal centres are transitory and easy to remove from the country (Gill, 2009). In the community, there is no reason to suggest the outcome of uncertainty is any different and is fully supported by the testimonies provided here.

Women who were asked to leave their provided accommodation completely were usually given little notice, and often had nowhere to go. They were at this point reliant on charities to house them. This is what had happened to Brenda, from earlier, who, when unable to find accommodation spent her nights sleeping on night buses in London. This option was suggested to her by charities who were unable to find space for her and advised her of the best routes for the practice suggesting this is a common solution for women in Brenda's situation. Riding buses was the safest option than some women could find. For example, Phoebe gave the address of her ex-partner to immigration when in detention to help secure her release. She was able to stay on his sofa for a few nights, but she explained how he lived with men who were selling drugs and that even he did not feel safe in their company.

Living with uncertainty in the community

Uncertainly was not confined to immigration detention, it also characterised the lives of women who had been released into the UK community. Women or men who leave immigration detention in the UK are rarely granted any long-term right to remain in the country. Instead, they are offered a far more provisional status of bail or temporary admission. In 2015, when the research for this book was conducted, only 30 of the 2,586 women who left detention were granted leave to enter or remain,[2] 1,398 were released on bail, 31 were released under the ambiguous category of 'other,' and 1,127 were removed from the country (around 44 per cent of people who were detained that year). The legal categories of bail, or (typically temporary) leave to enter or remain, mean that women remain uncertain about their futures for another indefinite period of time until the Home Office makes a decision on their immigration case. At this point, they may be granted some form of longer leave to remain, or they might be threatened again with removal from the country. All are at risk of being re-detained at any point.

The women I spoke with had lived in this uncertain state for between five months and six years. Only one participant, Phoebe, had received a positive decision from the Home Office with regard to her asylum case. Phoebe, who was from Kenya, had been moved onto a semi-permanent visa which allowed her the right to work and claim benefits when needed. She had two young children, aged around seven and two. She had been pregnant with her elder daughter when she was detained for three months. Her story is notable, as she was the only woman I interviewed in the community who was not struggling. All of the other women in the study had lived in the community waiting for a decision since their last stay in immigration detention. Some of the research participants had been detained more than once, in what can be a circular process going on some years. The ambiguity of their lives added another layer to already difficult situations. Women had no means to tell at what stage they were in their respective cases and most were anxiously waiting for long periods between updates from the Home Office. In the meantime, women were required to sign-on to the Home Office and were fearful of re-detention. Like the uncertainty of detention, such matters curtailed their independence and autonomy.

Understanding the immigration enforcement system in the UK

Women detailed in various ways how they were confused by the workings of the Home Office and immigration system in the UK, beginning with how they first came to the attention of the authority. Some women had escaped from traffickers and were guided to a reporting centre by a helpful member of the public. Others had been picked up and taken to detention on arrival at the airport, while still others had approached the Home Office in attempts to extend visas and were detained during this process. Whatever their circumstances leading up to detention, the women found the process of immigration enforcement confusing.

Nina, who had been married to her husband for 30 years, had lived with him in the UK for 4 years prior to her first confrontation with the Home Office. Nina was a victim of domestic violence perpetrated by her husband and the marriage had failed. She had returned to her family in her home country but had not confessed to them that she and her husband had divorced. On realising the restrictions her family would place on her when they understood she was no longer married, she attempted to return to the UK. She did not realise her spousal visa was now invalid and she was stopped at the airport and detained in Yarl's Wood for seven months. Nina described her reaction to this development:

> I am coming here like a blind person, I am no have idea … the woman they have strong right here, the woman she here, the solicitor they said you have right to come because your visa still working. About this I still come back here. When I came here they never mention what they do, they put you in detention and they say it is very good, lots of people detained, but you keep my freedom and my right, what is this?

Nina had expected the UK to be helpful, but found herself in what felt like a prison. Her case was further complicated by the responses she had given at the border, when she had failed to mention the history of domestic violence. In later interactions with the Home Office, her story regarding the violence she suffered from her husband was disbelieved as she had not initially disclosed the fact immediately on arrival to the UK. In her work on victims of gendered violence, Canning notes that a culture of disbelief within the Home Office is a common problem for women seeking asylum (Canning, 2017). Women's stories are often not believed, based on apparent discrepancies in their accounts. Yet, the work of Smith for Freedom from Torture (2004) and Muggeridge and Maman (2011) for Asylum Aid suggest that many inconsistencies in the accounts of women seeking asylum are the result of poor interviewing practices by the Home Office.

In the case of Nina, her responses were accurate at the time she made them. Upon re-entry to the UK her family were unaware of her divorce and she was no longer with her husband. However, after her ex-husband found she was in detention he informed her family of the divorce, and told them she was now in prison in the UK. It was only then that the trouble and threats from her family began.

The confusion felt by women regarding immigration enforcement in the UK can be highlighted by their admissions that they were completely unaware of the most basic ways of life in Britain, let alone the intricacies of the asylum system. Amy, who was trafficked to the UK for sex, should never have been detained.[3] She spent six months in the UK before she managed to escape from her traffickers, who had kept her inside at an address in London. She was helped to report to the Home Office by a member of the public who found her on the streets of London and offered her assistance. She had come from a remote village in her home country, and was not used to electricity or running water. She was unaware how to use a mobile phone, let alone what asylum was and how she could claim it. She was detained for a month until her experiences of trafficking were flagged up during her asylum interview. Amy was not clear why she was released or how. While in theory she understood that women who had been trafficked like her should not be detained, she had seen other women in detention with similar experiences who were not released. The only way she could understand her release was to describe it as magic:

> They don't have to like do anything, we been here, myself, when I got release they say maybe is it magic. Is it British magic that brought me out, I don't even know because I have no idea how they got me released because people have been there, good people is in there, people with terrible things but yet they will keep you there.

It is clear from Amy's experience that the unclear nature of immigration enforcement allowed little room for her to assert any agency in what happened to her. By ignoring the cultural differences of women from different nations around the world any autonomy they may have had is disallowed, making it easier for the Home Office to assert its powers to detain and remove individuals.

The threat of re-detention

Although released, women were not free from the Home Office, instead they had to report regularly at an immigration office in their general area. At the reporting centre, they often waited in long queues to have their name checked off on a computer system. The regularity of visits varied, typically becoming less regular the longer women had been waiting for a decision from the Home Office. Women were usually required to report once a week soon after released, and then this was revised to once a fortnight, once a month, and in one case a participant who had been waiting five years to receive a final decision reported once every six months and had been doing so for two years at the time that I spoke with her.

Women were terrified of signing on. It was not uncommon for women to be taken to detention without warning upon reporting to the Home Office and a few had experienced this already when they were first detained. Ryane explained in vivid detail the rising anxiety women described in the lead up to signing on:

> anytime I want to go and report I have this anxiety, depression on me and thinking oh god, I just want to go and report and come out, I don't want to be detained.

Any delay or problem with computer systems were an added stress, and Ryane went on to explain how one day the system was down when she went to report:

> you see me sweating, having, shaking, my heart went like … up and and I am just praying not to have this high blood pressure, because I am too young to have that kind of thing. So I was just sweating, oh god, you see me, I was shaking. It's really hard, it's really hard.

Another technique used by the Home Office to detain men and women is known as a morning raid. A number of women in this study had been detained in such a manner. In these instances, women are woken early in the morning by a team of enforcement officers who will take individuals to detention. Renas described the terror of this practice:

> So, when they come to me in the morning, at about half past 7, I was sleeping in my room. Then suddenly while I am sleeping I heard some people behind the door, try to open the door and I heard them, they talk with each other. Then, I wake up, but my room it was very dark because half past seven in the winter, and so suddenly they enter to my room and they switch on the light. Then I saw police, many police, I shocked, I thought I am, this was nightmare, or dream. Then I couldn't move, I couldn't say anything I couldn't catch myself in bed.

This practice, and all other acts of unexpected detention left a lasting, negative impression. Women were scared. The threat of re-detention was a constant looming threat for all the women in this study who remained in the UK, and made them feel that they were never really free from incarceration. Even Phoebe, who had received her right to remain described how she was still easily startled when someone knocked on her door. She also had an aversion to the sound of heavy boots, the rattling of keys, and ringing phones – sounds she had heard in immigration detention. Though now free from immigration control, the feeling of captivity had never truly left her.

The legacy of detention

The stories from participants were overwhelming in their sadness and included description of extreme stress, anxiety, and depression. Eight of the twelve women interviewed for this study were undergoing regular therapy sessions to help them cope with their experiences since arriving in the UK, and all women described mental unrest from anxiety through to suicidal ideation and depression more generally. Not all problems with mental health could be blamed purely on their time in detention; but women were clear that even if detention did not cause their problems, it certainly exacerbated existing troubles. The description of depression which had developed in detention was very similar in women in the community than that described by women who were in detention at the time of interview. However, women in the community were able to discuss these feelings in retrospect, which highlighted how painful the memories remained for them.

The depression they experienced in detention did not go away upon release. Instead, feelings of distress from detention became compounded by the continuing hardship and restriction faced by women while waiting for a decision from the Home Office. Women found it difficult to speak about their time in detention because it reminded them of painful memories. This was summarised by Micah, who I first met in detention:

> when I talk about that I really start to remember everything and I start to cry you know, and it make me so pain, so I try sometimes to not talk about that you know, because I stress myself more and more you know

A number of participants described how they tried to avoid talking about detention, and had only agreed to an interview in the hope that it would help others who might be detained in the future. This was also reflected in the refusals to be interviewed I received from women I approached to be interviewed for this project. The prospect of speaking about detention was simply too painful for some women.

Though some women were able to avoid talking about detention in their daily lives, avoiding thoughts of detention were not feasible. Ryane explained how detention crept into her daily life and caused her nightmares: 'Even me, I can never, this experience can never leave me. It can never leave me at all. It is like, sometimes if I sleep, it is like the reflection is coming back. You understand?' Ryane was so distressed during her time in detention she had tried to commit suicide. In our interview she showed me several scars caused by her attempts and described her fear of going mad there: 'I can't stay, I can't eat, I can't have fresh air, I can't, it's like everything in my life is just upside down.'

Intrusive thoughts were common, and women reported crying easily, severe apathy, and isolating themselves from others, alongside clinically diagnosed mental health disorders of depression and PTSD. Women believed that they would never be able to forget their time in detention and that it would shape how they lived for the remainder of their lives.

In attempts to stave off their symptoms of mental distress women tried to keep busy in the community. Yet, even if they were able to obtain funds to travel or attend college, they often found it hard to concentrate. Some described memory loss. Amy attended a local college and though English was her first language found herself unable to understand the classes:

> I am so so struggling. Like, at times it's something I know how to spell, but I can't. Sometimes I can't spell properly, and I am just like struggling to go into the college. I try to like, engage myself in so many things, but like, bring myself to who I am, no. I am finding it so so hard to be honest with you.

Renas, an academic in her own country, suffered from severe memory loss and apathy. She described how she suffered from chronic tiredness, which she partially blamed on the medication she was taking to deal with the depression she had suffered since her time in detention:

> I don't like this, my medication, I want to leave it. It make me very lazy and my memory, makes my memory become very terrible. Many time I lost my laptop, my phone, my money, so now the staff here, every time when they see me, they ask me 'keep your things! keep your bag!' Yeah, believe me, because many time, yesterday, also I lost my phone and in the class then come back, then come back in my class. Two months ago I lost my laptop on the seat, I left it. So, every week I lose it. So this affect too much on my memory.

Ryane felt that she had been fundamentally changed by her time in detention and then under Home Office restrictions in the community. She felt that if she had been deported quickly, she would have had a better chance at surviving at home, despite threats to her life she felt she faced there. However, with the depression that she now suffered she believed she had been broken mentally by the Home Office, and if she were to now return home, she would be unable to cope. Renas made similar accusations against the Home Office, detailing a series of losses to herself that she blamed on the organisation:

> They make my situation worse, my depression, my ability, my memory, all this effect on my body … I lost my health, my healthy, my ability to think right way. I lost my hobby, my situation not like this. My confidence I lost, I lost my confident. They like they kill us from inside. If you could you by any way this be easier, easier, cause they kill you from inside. So they are criminal, more than they kill me by knife or gun.

The loss and change of self, described here by Ryane and Renas, reflect the works of Coffey et al, who similarly found people released from immigration detention in Australia experienced negative transformations of themselves as a result of their incarceration (Coffey et al., 2010). Likewise, the substantial personal losses described here replicate the consequences of violations to dignity described by Jacobson (2009, 2010) in the opening chapters of this book.

Explaining distress post-detention

Women in the community were greatly offended by their detention and continued to feel the impact of their time there long after it had drawn to a close. They had time to reflect on their experiences of detention upon release and were able to articulate quite clearly why it had offended them so deeply. Detention, they were clear, was unjust and unfair. They had been treated like criminals, when all they wanted was sanctuary. The ongoing experiences in the community while awaiting a decision from the Home Office reinforced their sense that the government of the UK thought them to be of a lesser status than their own citizens, consequently diminishing their own sense of themselves. This status, they said, felt less than human.

Women believed they had spent time in a prison, and since their release the ongoing reporting to the Home Office did little to disprove this perception. The enforced lifestyles led by women made them feel they were treated as though they had done something very wrong. Alongside the fear of re-detention women endured when going to report, they also felt they were being monitored like they could not be trusted in the community. Nina described to me, through a friend who had come along to help translate, what it was like to be in this situation:

> But even when I go there I feel bad like they are looking at her like a criminal or something, they don't respect you and yeah, still feel scared when she go there because of the shock of detention is still in her mind.

When prompted to elaborate on how being treated like a criminal made her feel, Nina responded through her friend: 'She said it was feeling like really down, like, the way how they treat her was like, like they were killing her every single day, every single minute so, it was like horrible.' Nina also described the treatment of other women as proof of the Home Office's lack of care towards people in her situation. Travelling to report was often a substantial effort and though some women were provided with means to travel to reporting centres others were not and had to beg or borrow funds to make the trip. The lack of care evidenced by inflexible reporting arrangements added to women's sense that the Home Office regarded them as suspicious and untrustworthy. Their regular trips to report sentences also served as a constant reminder that their lives remained under the control of the government.

Women were also made to feel like criminals by former friends and associates due to their detention and ongoing involvement with the Home Office. Women were sometimes rejected by others because people assumed they had committed a serious crime. Larissa was surprised to be rejected by former friends on her return to the community. She explained how she had called a friend once she was released and found she was refusing her calls. Through a mutual friend she discovered her former friend was scared to speak with her 'Because I was in that place and she scared of me.' I asked if she might be scared due to her own immigration status, but Larissa clarified her former friend was here legally so it was not linked. Though Larissa had committed no crime, the stigma placed upon her by members of the community resulted in real consequences to her ability to actively participate in society.

Other women were rejected by family members in their home countries who could not understand the difference between a detention centre and prison. Women feared the stigma that may be placed on their families at home if their communities believed they had been imprisoned in the UK and many tried to hide their detention for this reason. This is a well-founded fear. In her work on the consequences of crime for relatives of prisoners, Condry illustrates how families of offenders are in fact vicariously shamed and share in the negative consequences of stigmatisation faced by serious offenders (Condry, 2007). That the women in this study had not committed a serious offence did not matter, as exemplified by Goffman in his original works on stigma, it is the perception of a tainted identity that is the defining feature of acceptance or not to society (Goffman, 1963).

The treatment experienced by women throughout the entire immigration enforcement process felt severely unjust. For those picked up during a dawn raid this process of injustice began here. Phoebe described how she felt when officers came to her home:

> You see like now, when they come for me, to get me to arrest me. I was not a criminal. Why are they bringing eight officers? They bringing those 8 officers to come arrest me. Everyone was looking

> on the window to see who is this criminal. It was so unfair, there is nothing I have done, I have only stay in the country illegally.

Women were unable to reconcile their treatment, 'as criminals,' with the way in which they felt they should be treated 'as humans.' Larissa experienced severe distress after her detention and linked this to her feelings of injustice:

> I felt that I didn't deserve, I felt why did it happen to me? I felt that I deserve much better in the future than that one, because like, I struggle. I tried my best, I never stole anything here, and it shouldn't, it just not good place for me.

She described how, though she had escaped further pain caused by detention itself, she still suffered from substantial psychological unrest after:

> So, for another one month, two months, I am still stressed out. First month, two months was terrible still. I was buying beer every day, drinking it. Crying, like crying when I am at home on my own. I used to go to a park, I was running fast and people were telling me, girl take it easy!

The pain of their experience was especially vivid for women who were seeking asylum. For Ryane, the pain of detention was linked to her inability to understand why she would be imprisoned when she had asked for help: 'I come here for safety, for the government to help me, and they are putting me in even more depressed. You understand, it is not good at all.'

Clara had come to the UK after fleeing from an abusive husband. She was offered passage with a trafficker, but only able to flee if she left her children behind. She already suffered from mental health problems before detention, and these issues had worsened severely when she was in detention. She was taking medication for PTSD when interviewed. She described a change in her identity after detention, where she no longer felt herself:

> My head was just so full of a lot of things. I was crying, I asked myself why? I have come to this country for safety. Why all this trauma? Why all this traumatising? Why are they traumatising?

> Why are they doing all this, all this things. I don't know if it is political or not, just thinking oh you are lying, you are lying, you are.

All of the women interviewed for this project felt their treatment at the hand of the Home Office was disproportionately harsh. This is especially true of women who applied for asylum as soon as they were physically possible as per the rules and guidelines set for persons seeking asylum. The feeling that the Home Office would then treat them in a way that was unfair and unjust made them feel they had done something wrong, and this led to substantial lessening of already damaged feelings of self-worth and self-esteem.

Gender and the experience of border control in the community

The deprivation, restriction, vilification, and injustice women felt post-detention and during their wait for a decision from the Home Office were not necessarily related to their gender, and men who have been released undergo similar experiences (Hasselberg, 2016; Klein and Williams, 2012). There were, however, some experiences that were related to being a woman. Some participants in the study had been trafficked to the UK for sex work. A number of women in the project were mothers. Some had children they had left during their escape to the UK, and others had children that were born here. Relationships with their offspring resulted in exceptional circumstances. Linked to this was a vulnerability to sub-optimal relationships in the hope of protection and to remain in the UK.

Home Office policy dictates that people who are victims of trafficking should not be held in immigration detention (Home Office, 2016), and do human rights protections ratified by the UK such as the UN High Commissioner 'guidelines on the applicable criteria and standards relating to the detention of asylum-seekers and alternatives to detention' (UNHCR, 2013). As has been described elsewhere in some detail, the detention of women who have been trafficked is especially damaging to their mental and physical health (BID, 2005; Canning, 2014, 2017; Girma et al., 2014, 2015; Medical Justice, 2012). The reality, however, is that victims of trafficking still find themselves incarcerated and the onus is them to prove their innocence (Canning, 2017). This was the case for at least four of the women that were interviewed for this project.

Women recounted how they had come to the UK, in the hope of a better life and/or to escape violent husbands. They were not aware they would be forced into prostitution. Some had spent long periods locked in houses forced into this role. Others, though not locked in were just as unwillingly forced into their situation. Ryane, who fled her country due to a risk to her life, explained how she had no choice:

> So the lady that traffic me, here in this country ask me to pay her money because she brought me here with money, so I had to pay her the money. So I don't have any choice but to pay to work with her.

To be placed in detention after suffering through this, and to endure long periods waiting in uncertainty were especially damaging for this group of women. Brenda, eloquently explained the way in which her suffering continued post-detention, and the impact it was having on her:

> I have reached the extent of saying why am I suffering in this world like this? I have suffered at home. I have suffered in detention. Now I am suffering where I am here. So you see, I am being squeezed, I am nearly bursting.

Brenda was unable to reconcile the suffering she had been through with their treatment in the UK. Like most women, Brenda believed the UK to be a place of rights and safety. Her resulting treatment was a shock. Likewise, Amy described how she believed British people would be kind and caring. She referred to the relative treatment as 'hell.'

Two of the women interviewed for this project post-release had been pregnant during their time in detention. The legacy of detention for them was an especially hard memory, and their release back into the community was especially difficult as expecting mothers. Neither felt they had been cared for appropriately in detention and both had feared they would lose their babies as a result. Their experiences are reflected in works from NGOs (see Medical Justice, 2013; Girma et al., 2014; Girma et al., 2015) and the Shaw report into vulnerable persons in detention (Shaw, 2016), who all agreed pregnant women should not be held in detention. Pregnant women are now expected to be released from detention within 72 hours of the Home Office confirming their pregnancy; however, at the time of this research the law and guidelines had yet to be established. Phoebe was still in her first trimester when she was taken into detention and spent three months there:

> Let's say for 3 months, and for every place, you are pregnant, depressed. It was too much, it was too hard … so it was like, I remember it was this Christmas, it was Christmas time and pregnant so it was so hard for me, because it was a proper stress. Stress was too much.

Julie missed her 20-week anomaly scan because she was in detention.[4] She was fearful that her child was ill and told me the only medical care she had for her child was through an external organisation called Medical Justice who she contacted personally. Medical Justice, in turn, sent a midwife to her in the centre to check on the baby. Nonetheless, Julie blames the detention centre for the excess stress she felt during her pregnancy and worried what impact that may have had on her child's development. Julie found her time in detention traumatising due to the pregnancy and had contemplated suicide when she felt she could not cope with the stress:

> something tell me to suicides you know because you have so problem, you have so stress, you don't know what you can do, you have baby inside you, you scared too much you want to say, I want to kill by myself. Kill by my self family. Kill by myself.

Both women were released before the birth of their children, but additional problems meant their release was not straight forward. Phoebe was released to inappropriate housing, having used the address of her former partner to ensure she would be released. She was unable to stay for long as he shared a house with other men who she felt unsafe around. She was ultimately moved to a town she had never heard of and after spending some time in a hostel was moved to a shared house. Julie was similarly released to hostel accommodation, and though she was late in her pregnancy was told she could not move to a shared house until after the child was born. She was helped by a charity to find accommodation in between but had since been moved to a shared house. She was unhappy in this accommodation and told me how the other residents sometimes told her they did not like her and her baby living there.

Another participant had become pregnant since leaving their incarceration. Micah had begun a relationship with a friend very soon after leaving Yarl's Wood and had quickly fallen pregnant. Micah had complex health problems that had been exacerbated during detention, including epilepsy. She had been told by her doctor that she needed to take care of herself and remain calm and relaxed during the pregnancy. She was trying her best, but often felt low and found herself crying easily when she remembered her time in detention and the possibility of being re-detained:

> it's like I am scared something because I don't know which minute, what is going to happen. Like I thank god, I am taking the tablets you know, and I just, so it is a little bit stop because I have quiet time, you know like I try to forget you know, all that things. But of course I can't.

When she was first pregnant Micah believed the Home Office could not detain her due to the fact, however at the time this was only a rumour, and she had since worried again she might be re-detained regardless.

Micah was lucky enough to be in a relationship with a partner who helped to care for her during her pregnancy. This was not the case for most women, however. Phoebe explained how she became pregnant with her second child. She felt her confidence had been lost during detention and her time waiting for temporary admission to the country. She had been helped by a charity to complete courses to help her confidence, but was plagued by feelings of guilt about some of the things she had done to stay in the country. She had spent time in relationships with men she believed did not respect her, after they had offered to help her and her first child. She had another child with one man, because she believed he would continue to help her if she gave him a child. Though she knew this was not the right thing to do she felt she needed help and this was one of very few options available.

Conclusion

Women, when released from detention, face a different form of imprisonment. Although they are free from the physical walls, gates, and barbed wire they found so offensive in removal centres, they face another regime characterised by uncertainty and restriction that shadows their time in detention. Unsurprisingly then, the women interviewed in the community suffered from serious mental health problems such as anxiety, stress, depression, PTSD, confusion, and loss of memory. They were all adamant their ailments were exacerbated or caused by detention and made worse by their continued treatment in the community.

Women in the community were, to some extent, the most anxious and vulnerable of all the groups I interviewed. While some of the pains women were enduring related to the impact of their period in detention, many were specific to their precarious position within the community. Still denied access to the protections of citizenship, their sense of themselves as humans was undermined, and as such their sense of dignity continued to be challenged.

Notes

1 Most women I interviewed stated they were seeking asylum, but this was not always the case, and some were not able to express to me what exactly they were waiting on a decision for.
2 Notably, leave to enter or remain is also not a guarantee of a long-term or permanent stay in the UK, but the recipient is usually able to live free of the Home Office until a date in the future where the recipient either makes their status permanent or must again enter the cycle of application for leave to remain.
3 Based on the UN High Commissioner 'guidelines on the applicable criteria and standards relating to the detention of asylum-seekers and alternatives to detention' that if an individual has been tortured in the past, or if they are a victim of trafficking they should not be detained as it is considered too damaging (UNHCR, 2013), and the Home Office's own guidance on adults at risk in immigration detention (Home Office, 2016).
4 The 20-week anomaly scan is a key milestone for pregnancy care in the UK. It is at this point doctors are able to identify anomalies of the foetus and set in motion any medical care required for the continuing health of the mother and child.

References

Allsopp J, Sigona N and Phillimore J (2014) *Poverty among Refugees and Asylum Seekers in the UK an Evidence and Policy Review*. IRiS Working Paper Series: 1–46.

BID (2005) *Fit to Be Detained? Challenging the Detention of Asylum Seekers and Migrant with Health Needs*. London: Bail for Immigration Detainees.

British Red Cross and Boaz Trust (2013) *A Decade of Destitution: Time to Make a Change*. Manchester: British Red Cross and Boaz Trust.

Canning V (2010) Who's human? Developing sociological understandings of the rights of women raped in conflict. *International Journal of Human Rights* 14(6): 849–864. https://doi.org/10.1080/13642987.2010.512127.

Canning V (2014) Women, asylum and the harms of detention. *Criminal Justice Matters* 98(1): 10–11.

Canning V (2017) *Gendered Harm and Structural Violence in the British Asylum System*. Abingdon: Routledge. https://doi.org/10.4324/9781315720975.

Coffey GJ, Kaplan I, Sampson RC and Tucci MM (2010) The meaning and mental health consequences of long-term immigration detention for people seeking asylum. *Social Science and Medicine* 70(12): 2070–2079. https://doi.org/10.1016/j.socscimed.2010.02.042.

Condry R (2007) *Families Shamed: The Consequences of Crime for Relatives of Serious Offenders*. Cullompton: Willan Publishing.

Doyle L (2009) *"I Hate Being Idle" Wasted Skills and Enforced Dependence among Zimbabwean Asylum Seekers in the UK*. London: Refugee Council. Refugee Council.

Fekete L (2001) The emergence of Xeno racism. *Race & Class* 43(2): 23–40. https://doi.org/10.1007/978-1-4471-0517-6_4.

Gill N (2009) Governmental mobility: The power effects of the movement of detained asylum seekers around Britain's detention estate. *Political Geography* 28(3): 186–196. https://doi.org/10.1016/j.polgeo.2009.05.003.

Girma M, Radice S, Tsangarides N, et al. (2014) *Detained: Women Asylum Seekers Locked up in the UK* London: Women for Refugee Women, pp. 1–48.

Girma M, Kershaw I, Lousley G, et al. (2015) *I Am Human: Refugee Women's Experiences of Detention in the UK*. London: Women for Refugee Women.

Goffman I (1963) *Stigma: Notes on the Management of Spoiled Identity*. Harmondsworth: Penguin.

Griffiths M (2013) Living with uncertainty: Indefinite immigration detention. *Journal of Legal Anthropology* 1(3): 263–286. https://doi.org/10.4059/jla.2013.2616.

Griffiths M (2014) Out of time: The temporal uncertainties of refused asylum seekers and immigration detainees. *Journal of Ethnic and Migration Studies* 40(12): 1991–2009. https://doi.org/10.1080/1369183X.2014.907737.

Hamilton K and Harris J (2009) *21 Days Later: Destitution and the Asylum System*. London: The Refugee Survival Trust and British Red Cross.

Hasselberg I (2016) *Enduring Uncertainty: Deportation, Punishment and Everyday Life*. Oxford: Berghahn.

Home Office (2016) *Immigration Act 2016: Guidance on Adults at Risk in Immigration Detention*. London: Home Office.

Jacobson N (2009) A taxonomy of dignity: A grounded theory study. *BMC International Health and Human Rights* 9: 3. https://doi.org/10.1186/1472-698X-9-3.

Jacobson N (2010) *Dignity and Health*. Nashville: Vanderbilt University Press.

Klein A and Williams L (2012) Immigration detention in the community: Research on the experiences of migrants released from detention centres in the UK. *Population, Space and Place* 18(6): 741–753. https://doi.org/10.1002/psp.1725.

Liebling A (2004) *Prisons and their Moral Performance: A Study of Values, Quality and Prison Life*. Oxford: Oxford University Press.

Liebling A and Maruna S (2005) *The Effects of Imprisonment*. Collumpton: Willan.

Madan TN (1992) Dying with dignity. In: *Social Science and Medicine*, pp. 425–432. https://doi.org/10.1016/0277-9536(92)90335-N.

Medical Justice (2012). *'The Second Torture': The Immigration Detention of Torture Survivors*. London: Medical Justice.

Medical Justice (2013) *Expecting Change: The Case for Ending the Detention of Pregnant Women*. London: Medical Justice.

Miller AB and Keys CB (2001) Understanding dignity in the lives of homeless persons. *American Journal of Community Psychology* 29(2): 331–355.

Moore LW and Miller M (1999) Initiating research with doubly vulnerable populations. *Journal of Advanced Nursing* 30(5): 1034–1040. https://doi.org/10.1046/j.1365-2648.1999.01205.x.

Muggeridge H and Maman C (2011) *Unsustainable: The quality of initial decision-making in women's asylum claims*. London: Asylum Aid. Available at: http://d2ihhomkd2yhtk.cloudfront.net/wp-content/uploads/2013/02/unsustainableweb.pdf.

Mulvey G (2009) *'Even among Asylum Seekers we are the Lowest': Life on Section 4 Support in Glasgow*. Glasgow: Scottish Refugee Council.

Phillimore J, Thornhill J, Latif Z, et al. (2010) *Delivering in an Age of Super-Diversity: West Midlands Review of Maternity Services for Migrant Women*. London: Department of Health.

Refugee Action (2006) *The Destitution Trap: Asylum's Untold Story*. London: Refugee Action.

Sautier LP, Vehling S and Mehnert A (2014) Assessment of patients' dignity in cancer care: Preliminary psychometrics of the German version of the patient dignity inventory (PDI-G). *Journal of Pain and Symptom Management* 47(1): 181–188. https://doi.org/10.1016/j.jpainsymman.2013.02.023.

Shaw S (2016) *Review into the Welfare in Detention of Vulnerable Persons: A Report to the Home Office by Stephen Shaw*. London: HMSO, CM9186.

Singer R (1972) Privacy, autonomy, and dignity in the prison: A preliminary inquiry concerning constitutional aspects of the degradation process in our prisons. *Buffalo Law Review* 21(2): 669–716.

Smith E (2004) *Right First Time? Home Office Asylum Interviewing and Reasons for Refusal Letters*. London: Medical Foundation for the Care of Victims of Torture (Now Freedom from Torture). https://doi.org/10.21037/atm.2016.08.52.

Turnbull S (2016) 'Stuck in the middle': Waiting and uncertainty in immigration detention. *Time and Society* 25(1): 61–79. https://doi.org/10.1177/0961463X15604518.

UNHCR (2013) *Guidelines on the Applicable Criteria and Standards Relating to the Detention of Asylum-Seekers and Alternatives to Detention*. Geneva: UNHCR.

4

REMOVAL

The final stage of research undertaken for this book was with women removed from the UK and taken to Jamaica, where 26 women took part. Interviews were undertaken in Jamaica, where the women had been removed to, either under Immigration Act powers or following a criminal conviction. Jamaica and the UK have a long history spanning back to the British colonisation of the country, which lasted from 1655 until 1962. During the 1950s, substantial numbers of Jamaicans entered the UK without restriction (Foner, 1985; Thomas-Hope, 2002; Tidrick, 1966), including some who entered on special schemes under which they were brought over to fill gaps in NHS nursing positions after the Second World War (Batnitzky and McDowell, 2011; Brown, 1997). The Commonwealth Immigrants Act of 1962 brought in restrictions for Jamaicans and other former colonial subjects seeking to enter the UK; however, Britain remains a popular destination (Golash-Boza, 2015).

Since this research was conducted in 2015, the generation of Jamaicans and people from other Caribbean countries who immigrated to the UK have become commonly referred to as the Windrush generation, named after one of the cruise liners which transported large groups of men and women from the Caribbean in the 1950s. This name is now synonymous with the wrongful deportation of men and women from the UK to Jamaica. However, at the time of this research, the Windrush scandal had not yet come to light. It is very likely that the narratives in this chapter would have been different after this story broke in 2018. I have returned to my data to determine if any of the women who

DOI: 10.4324/9780367823153-5

participated in this study were of this generation, and they were not. I cannot confidently say the same of the women interviewed in immigration detention at the time, though there were women who were of an age that it was plausible.

Thematically, the concerns of women once removed were fundamentally different to those still living under the conditions imposed by the Home Office. They were free from incarceration, they had the freedom to find their own employment, and were not at risk of re-detention. Yet, the legacy of their time under UK immigration enforcement control still caused substantial, and disproportionate, trouble in their lives. Women returned to Jamaica wanted to be treated fairly, justly, and with respect for their personal circumstances. Instead, they experienced persistent violations to their dignity across all spheres of their lives; women were labelled and stigmatised when they returned to Jamaica, they were considered 'criminal' and treated as such. Many discovered that their previous circle of friends and family were much less willing to offer their support than they had expected and hoped. Women found it challenging to look respectable, support their children, or gain employment, and as a consequence, their sense of self-worth suffered. Some had also been deeply offended by the treatment they received from the UK government during the process of their removal. Combining all these aspects, they described to me a set of circumstances in which it was difficult, if not impossible, to maintain their sense of self-worth. As will become clear, those who had spent time in prison in the UK had better outcomes than those who had only spent time in immigration detention, raising important questions about the relative punishing effect of these two sites that will be discussed in conclusion.

Living as a 'returned' citizen

All people removed or returned to Jamaica faced a hostile welcome from their communities. Women were labelled as 'deportees' and 'criminals' due to their status as returned migrants and stigmatised as such. The returned population of men and women are uniformly considered to be 'deportees' by those in the local community and this label, women complained, over-rode their individual qualities and experiences. Daloris had spent three years in prison in the UK after agreeing to carry drugs for a friend. She was 21 years old when she left, and had agreed to carry them because she desperately wanted to travel. She had a five-year-old son at the time of the offence, who remained behind in the care of his aunt. Daloris explained to me the way people categorised women and men on their return:

> People label you as deportee. So, somebody will see you and say that deportee boy that is deportee girl or that and they get deport. People classify you and put you into a little box by yourself as deportee.

Although women tried to hide their immigration status to avoid this categorisation, their attempts were rarely successful. Cassandra had spent 14 years in the UK before she was returned to Jamaica. For most of this time, she had a valid student visa and survived by working 20 hours a week alongside her studies. She was detained and ultimately removed in 2014 after she tried to change her student visa to an 'unmarried partner' visa. Cassandra explained to me the reaction of people in her community when they discovered she had been deported:

> You know when I tell people they have a funny reaction about deportee or something. You can't tell everybody because they will start to label you as that. Cause even if they know your name, they won't call you by your name. They say 'deportee, deportee.' They call plenty people like that.

Once labelled as a deportee, women recounted, they were shunned by former communities, looked down on, and treated as though they belonged to an underclass. In some cases, stigma left women in fear for their safety and that of their children after intimidation from gangs. Malene had spent 11 years in the UK, she had moved there after the birth of her daughter. Although she had been in stable employment before she fell pregnant, she had been unable to work since her daughter was born and received little support from the child's father. She left for the UK to provide a better life for her daughter who remained behind with Malene's mother and sister. After her return Malene's daughter was threatened by gangs in the neighbourhood because of her status as a deportee and her failure to return with capital. The gang referred to Malene as 'naked' because she returned from the UK without any possessions: 'Yes and she saying that when people cursing me she don't like it, and they tell me why, your mother, she British and she have nothing.' Malene's daughter suffered the effects of vicarious stigmatisation because of the 'spoiled' status of her mother.

The impact of the label of 'deportee,' socially, was debilitating for women. Some tried to hide their status, to avoid being shunned, but this deception made it hard to build close relationships and left them socially isolated. It also required a relentless performance to appear 'normal' to others. Managing the stigma was hard. Many participants were depressed and described an overall loss of self-esteem (see also Turnbull, 2017). In addition, most of the women who participated in my research in Jamaica felt unable to seek support. Their shame was compounded by feeling they were unlikely to receive much needed help from former friends and unlikely to secure accommodation.

The problems caused by the deportee label related to the term's association with criminality.

Geographically, Jamaica is well-situated between places of cocaine production and the affluent markets of the UK and the United States (Clarke, 2006; Klein, Day, and Harriot, 2004). Nearly 20 years ago, the National Security Minister of Jamaica put the value of the drug trafficking racket in Kingston at approximately US$3–3.6 billion (Clarke, 2006). The use of people as 'mules' is still common. Individuals employed in this way conceal drugs, either in their own body or within their luggage (Clarke, 2006). The long history of drug trade and gangs in the Caribbean, and the forced return of a number of well-known gang leaders and members for their involvement in criminal activities (Miller, 2012), has resulted in the 'criminalisation' of nearly everyone who is returned to Jamaica. There is a widespread perception, however erroneous, among people in Jamaica that 'deportees' have committed crime overseas and an accompanying expectation that they will continue to commit crime on their return (Golash-Boza, 2015). In fact, while a number of those removed from overseas will have committed a criminal offence, there is no evidence to suggest this population is any more likely to commit a crime on return than the average Jamaican (Headley, 2006). Yet, such academic work has little effect on perceptions.

Eve offers a clear example of the situation many women described upon facing their new identity as criminal. Eve had lived in London for four years. She was returned to Jamaica when she was unable to produce evidence of a right to be in the UK during a chance encounter with the police. She described passionately the way she had been labelled not only as a 'deportee' but also as a criminal:

> You tell them, say, you come home, you remove, if you removed they say why they deport you? Cause them look at you

> one way, a criminal. You understand? You must be criminal, CRIMINAL!

Women like Eve felt vilified, shamed, and excluded from their communities. They also felt they were unimportant to other people because of it. They feared the negative social reaction of others, and went out of their way to avoid confrontation. Malene described her hopelessness:

> No, nobody really cares. Nobody cares. Nobody cares. I'm just there. Nobody cares. Nobody don't ask you how you feeling. What you doing? What you need? Nobody cares. I tell you the truth. If I'm really hungry, I am even scared to ask someone. Cause you know nobody, nobody cares.

Although half the sample of women in this study had not been 'deported' for criminal activity, but rather had been administratively removed, this made little difference to their experiences in Jamaica. Essentially, they were considered criminal by their local communities. Removal centres, like prisons, exacerbated the stigma of returned populations, as these spaces were perceived as punitive, and the people who had been detained within them seen as 'guilty' by association (see Turnbull, 2017, for similar findings).

Notwithstanding the numbers who are regularly sent back to Jamaica, the women's stories suggest that there was widespread unfamiliarity about the process of removal, or the complexity of immigration control in Britain. This is exemplified by Grace, who was 16 years old when she left Jamaica for the UK hoping to study. On arrival in Britain, she was declined entry. She was told her sponsors, which included her mother, had insufficient funds to support her. Grace was sent to a hotel near the airport for the night and told to return the next morning for a flight back to Jamaica. She left the hotel and went to her mother's home in London instead. During her time in the UK, Grace had worked her way up into the position of manager at a sports store in London. She explained how people misunderstood the process of removal:

> Some people tend to judge you, right, for instance when you come out there before and see me and people see me. People assume because you're deported you do something wrong.

> You're probably was in drugs or going for some foolishness or something, they don't understand you can just overstay and get deported.

Women who were in the same position as Grace, who had been removed due to a violation of immigration law, were particularly offended by the assumption they were criminal. Eve, introduced earlier, found her transition back to the Jamaican community so troubling she contemplated ending her own life and that of her children:

> Trust me, one day I plan[ned] to kill myself and kill the kids. The way I went through it, I ... it was rough. Trust me. I can't imagine, live here like 13 years. To come back, just because of your status ... to commit a crime, well that's different. But, when you came back because of your status ... it's not easy.

It was difficult to tell if Eve had truly contemplated ending her life or that of her children. When I spoke with her, I had no fear for her safety. However, her powerful testimony makes clear that she had struggled to reconcile how difficult her life had become due to what she felt was a minor offence. She resented being grouped with women who had carried drugs to the UK. Eve also believed people in her community would be more willing to help her out if they understood she was 'just' an 'illegal immigrant.'

Women who had been imprisoned for drug trafficking too, explained how they entered into agreements to carry drugs to the UK only because their choices had been restricted by their difficult life circumstances and limited options for survival. Women were typically blind to the consequences of being a drug mule if they were caught by the UK government. Naomi explained how the man who had offered her drugs had never explained the consequences of being caught with drugs or the risk to her life involved when swallowing drugs:

> He tell me that everything going to be alright. Somebody going to pick me up at the airport and I'm going to pass it out, give them, and then anywhere I want to go I can go. Yeah, he never tell me it was something serious otherwise I wouldn't do it! It when I reach up there that I find out it was so serious. And I never know that it could kill me, that it was put inside of me I would died! I never know those things.

Naomi was adamant that if she had known the consequences, she would not have agreed to carry the drugs. It is, however, not also a simple choice to decline a request to carry drugs, and a number of participants hinted at coercion in their descriptions of how they came to accept them. This is supported by other research with female smugglers (Bailey, 2013; Campbell, 2008; Esmee Fairbairn Foundation, 2003). Similarly, women described situations where they felt their only viable choice, in order to feed their family, was to accept the generous offer of money provided by smugglers. Olivia was a single mother to six children at the time of her offence, she explained how she was living in poverty:

> Well, I couldn't find meals for the kids, couldn't find clothing for the kids and I didn't want to turn to prostitution, you know? Or to steal anything from anybody, so I got the offer, so I took the offer.

Olivia knew she was carrying something to the UK 'for a friend' but she was not aware the package contained drugs, otherwise, she claimed, she too would not have taken the offer. It is, nonetheless, clear to see that the other options available, such as prostitution or theft, were perhaps more difficult to justify than questioning a generous offer that would support her and her children financially. On her return from the UK, Olivia defended her actions on these terms, and this defence provided her with a confidence to protect their sense of self-worth. Her story, Olivia explained, served as a warning for others:

> When I just came home it wasn't so welcome for me where I live, cause people pointing fingers at me, saying 'oh, prisoner' and all of that. But I didn't care. I'm proud because at the end of the day I make an example for others. You know?

The use of the term 'proud' here suggests the impact of labelling was minimised by Olivia's reaction to it. Women who could not justify why they had been returned felt especially wronged and vilified by the label they considered unfair and unjust.

Though some women have spent time in prison, they were still defiant about their criminal brand. They pointed out how unjust it was that the criminal label followed them home. Not only had their sentence finished, but as a number of them pointed out, they had never committed an offence in Jamaica and so they believed they should not be punished there. Jocelyn had spent four years in the UK, she was imprisoned after 'helping'[1] someone and falling into trouble with the police and removed after. She explained how a gentleman had come to the prison to explain that her criminal record would not follow her home to Jamaica:

> him say when you go back home police record won't come out there with us, but it come! So when I go by the police record, every time evidence, they put up something for you to work, your name come up on it and that is not fair.

Women's records were, however, marked upon their return to Jamaica. It was difficult to understand exactly how, and on what system, women's status as a 'returned' citizen was held, but the effect of the record had substantial implications for women's abilities to build back a life in Jamaica. Breona explained how she had been fingerprinted when she came through the airport in Jamaica, and the impact this had on her ability to find work: 'me can't get a job because of the fingerprints. Because we were fingerprinted at the airport here where we don't think we should be fingerprinted because we didn't do anything here.' Women explained to me that legitimate employers require record checks before work can begin and a number of women had either been declined work based on their record as a 'returned' person or had not tried to find such employment based on the perception of their ineligibility. Most also believed their national records[2] were marked and avoided applying for any position that required employment checks for this reason.[3] They lacked confidence to approach potential employers for fear they would be 'discovered' and discriminated against.

In July 2015, when the interviews for this project took place, the unemployment rate for women in Jamaica was 17.7 per cent[4] (Statistics Institute of Jamaica, 2016). In this already difficult job market women found that employers were unwilling to hire from a population considered undesirable. Many also faced age discrimination. In Jamaica employers can advertise for employees within an age range, and for women this range was typically under 35. This finding is supported by other researchers, who found employees in Jamaica between the ages of 45 and 65 were more likely to be fired, and less likely to be hired in the first instance (Mujtaba et al., 2006; Mujtaba et al., 2004). As such, very few of those I interviewed had secure employment. Most survived by utilising the informal urban economic markets of downtown Kingston and Montego Bay. Their utilisation of these markets allowed women to participate in money-making activities outside the formal economy, which they referred to as 'hustling.'[5] In Jamaica hustling practices range from the selling of goods on the street, wiping windscreens at red lights, and assisting tourists to carry their luggage to more creative service provisions such as the braiding of tourists' hair or similar. Women in the study appeared to favour the selling of goods, and described how they had to build up their stock of items over time. They would start with one or two pieces, such as a bottle of shampoo or roll of toilet paper, and when they sold them, they would use the profits to slowly accumulate a larger collection of items for sale. They hawked their wares on blankets and carts on Kingston's busy downtown streets.

A small number of women had become more successful vendors and ran market stalls or shops. They could make enough money to find accommodation and feed themselves and their families most of the time. However, increasing competition and economic instability meant even they had to top up their earnings by taking on additional work such as laundry or other service opportunities. Less successful hustlers or vendors rarely had enough to cover all their needs and so their income was supplemented by begging from friends and family. The practice of begging, however, was another source of shame for women in this study. Those who had lived in the UK had become accustomed to their role as provider for themselves and their children in Jamaica. These women were used to being independent and were proud of the help they could provide. Begging was an overwhelming, though necessary, departure from this role and the lack of autonomy it caused resulted in a great deal of distress.

Inability to secure meaningful employment and income for most of the women in the study resulted in circumstances of prolonged deprivation, poverty, and dependence. As described by Eve: 'Coming back here man, it's a struggle. Me come off the plane back home, me see poverty. Me see hungry, me see starvation, me see none how to live, me see all kinds of things. Yes.' The ongoing fight for survival was a common theme in the interviews. The story of Joanne epitomised the problems many faced. Joanne was 65 years old when I interviewed her. She had spent approximately 11 years in the UK before she was deported in 2014. In London, she had survived by catering for small parties and with the help of family and friends. Joanne contrasted her inability to manage her new life in Jamaica, with her previous situation in England where she had been independent and able to send money home. Joanne felt pained by the loss of her autonomy, especially when she resorted to begging for help. Furthermore, accommodation was difficult to find and expensive if women were unable to stay with family and friends. Joanne described to me her current accommodation in Jamaica:

> The place? It's like … it's not clean. The place is not clean. The drain blocked. Insects. Rubbish. You come in like dump, and you have to be squeezing in those kind of places. I cannot manage it, you understand me?

Some of the women returned to Jamaica had retained homes on the Island. These women, however, were returning after many years abroad and found their homes in various states of disrepair. Jocelyn, from earlier, had left her house in the care of her adult son and his cousin, and on return had found they had stolen anything of value and left the rest in disarray:

> Oh, I'd have my house that I leave. But everything was mash up. Everything. Jewellery, passbook, everything. Cause they never keep the place, them mash up my furniture and everything.

On return, Jocelyn was left with a house, but no possessions or furniture. Hers was one of the more optimistic accounts however, as she was able to obtain a small loan from the bank using the collateral from her home, which she used to start her small market stall.

In addition to accommodation problems, it was not unusual for women to go without food. Joanne, was initially living with her 24-year-old son, but was asked to move from the one-bedroom home in Kingston by her son's girlfriend. Her son continued to support her for a time, but he had since lost his job:

> Now he's not working. He would like help from me, but I can't even help myself … I don't remember sitting and eating anything warm for a month cause I don't have the money and he don't have it either.

Women found the struggle for food hard, particularly in relation to their former lives in the UK. Earlene had spent ten years working in London at various cleaning jobs. She had left four children in Jamaica, aged between 7 and 13 years old, and sent back money for them when she could. She discussed with me how she felt when remembering what her life was like in the UK:

> Sometime now looking in my fridge, the only thing I see here is a water bottle. You know? Sometimes I feel like I drink some milk, and I think, oh my God back in England you can get a big jug of milk for a pound. And out here, a little small box cost you 50 [JMD, ca £0.30] and you can't even buy it.

Earline and others continued to wonder if their lives would have been better if they had never left Jamaica. Such uncertainty about past choices caused them considerable anguish. The economic situation in Jamaica was perceived to have deteriorated in their absence, disadvantaging anyone who had not remained in employment throughout.

Joanne described the impact of this kind of economic deprivation. As a caterer in London, she had hoped to continue similar work on her return to Jamaica. She was, however, unable to raise enough money to cook regularly. Instead, she held a small market stall selling what goods she could find. Joanne's situation was additionally difficult as she felt threatened by a family member, whom she blamed for her son's death. Her inability to secure employment limited her ability to move away from the area that she was living in, close to this family member. Joanne found her situation infantilising, using the term 'big woman' which in Jamaican English describes an adult woman. She explained:

> I am not a child, I need to behave like a big woman, a big people life. I can't work. I can't think that the bad man there, go to the police … Anywhere I walk I have to look … last Saturday morning, I'm coming across a man, frightened with a gun at me. I cannot live those kind of life! I'm not used to that life when I'm in England! You understand? I can't manage it. I can't manage life out here.

The infantilisation felt here by Joanne can also be linked to a lack of autonomy. As an adult she would expect to have the means to move to a place of safety. That she was not able to was an offence to her sense of self as an adult and caused her to feel distressed.

Deportation vs administrative removal

Most of the women I spoke to in Jamaica had either smuggled drugs or had moved to the UK in search of work. Two became involved in drugs or other undisclosed criminality while in the UK. Half of the women had overstayed their visas, had then been detained in a removal centre, and subsequently removed. The other half had been caught with drugs on their arrival to the UK, served a prison sentence, and had then been deported. In effect, whether women fell into the 'prison' group or the 'overstayer' group, and the resulting circumstances surrounding their removal from the country, impacted their sense of dignity on return. Those who had carried drugs to the UK, were caught on arrival, and spent all their time in Britain in prison, described their treatment by UK authorities in more positive terms. These participants described their treatment as fair, and agreed it had been right to return them to Jamaica at the end of their sentence. In contrast, many of the women who had been removed from the UK after immigration-based offences, such as overstaying visas, had unresolved complaints concerning their return to Jamaica.

Women returned to Jamaica for immigration offences felt their expulsion from the country was unjust. This group included those who had spent as many as 13 years living in the UK. For working-class women in Jamaica, it is still commonplace to emigrate in search of employment, leaving behind children who are looked after by extended family members (Crawford-Brown, 1999; Thomas-Hope, 2002; Pottinger, 2005). Across the Eastern Caribbean more generally it is estimated that between 10 and 20 per cent of children live in households where at least one parent is absent due to migration (Blank, 2007). The ubiquity of this practice has led to the term 'barrel children,' named after the historical practice of sending home barrels of goods to children left behind by their mothers (Crawford-Brown, 1999; Dillon and Walsh, 2012). Half of the women I interviewed for this book fell into this category; they had emigrated to the UK in search of employment and before detention were sending home regular remittances to their children and their carers.

In this study, this particular group of women had substantial ties to the communities in which they lived in the UK, and they were hurt by the thought that they could be removed after such a long stay in the country. Earlene, who had spent ten years in London, described the offence she felt watching others with substantial links to the country removed:

> after 10 years or 15 years, cause you have people that been here for 15 or more, lots of years and I see ladies in there that is married!

> And they still send them home. Have children! And they still want to send them home.

Participants felt the government were indifferent to their individual circumstances, as they could not see how the government would remove them if they were aware of their personal connections. Consequently, women believed that they did not matter to the government and this impacted their feelings of self-importance. Eve felt the government should take into account the reason women move to the UK in the first place:

> Worst, most are women, because most are single mothers in Jamaica. When you leave your kids to come to next one's country, I'm not talking the trouble makers and the ones that don't want for anything, but, if up now and give them no problem, just get old and the system file says overstay, me think England should do a better job, give them a chance man, make them make the most of life, cause sometime it just life you want, better, help.

Most of the women in this study were single mothers, as Eve suggests, and had travelled to the UK because they had been unable to support themselves and their families in Jamaica. They described the cruelty of the lack of compassion they encountered. Women who had not committed a criminal offence struggled to comprehend why they were being made to leave. Participants could understand why those who had trafficked drugs or were involved in other crime were not wanted in the UK, but took offence to the idea that they were also not welcome. Not only had they caused no trouble in the UK, but many reported that they had made great efforts to participate fully in their adopted community. Cassandra felt the government should have taken into account her contributions to society over the 14 years she had lived in the UK:

> They could have give you a chance because you are there for so long. But they didn't give that to me. Because I was on the system, I used to pay my tax, I was working in a health organisation, I was working in a hospital.

Many of the women who had been administratively removed had never attempted to 'hide' from the government, they were fully registered on government systems, such as HMRC,[6] as described by Cassandra, and working openly in organisations such as the National Health Service (NHS). The refusal of extending visas often came as a surprise, along with the subsequent removal. They were, effectively, easy targets for the government to remove as a result of their keenness to fully participate in their adoptive community and country. It is this sentiment exactly that caused offence to their dignity, as women witnessed 'other' people from countries outside the UK remaining in the UK, despite behaviour they considered to be 'trouble.' Nyesha explained how she felt the Home Office was removing the wrong people:

> I think once you are there you are not giving them any trouble, there are people there that gives trouble, and I always wonder, they are so arrogant and rude and yet the Home Office didn't seek them out.You are there to try to do the right thing. Obey all the laws and rules and you are the ones that are being picked up.

Nyesha had left Jamaica to escape an abusive relationship. She lived for three years in the UK by extending her student visa lawfully. When the Home Office declined to offer her another renewal, she began a lengthy appeal and reapplication process. She explained to me how she spent the next eight years in the UK fighting to stay through appeals and the courts. In 2010, she was asked to sign on, attending the Home Office regularly so they were able to check her whereabouts. In 2012, while still signing on, she was invited for an interview and told her application had been denied six months earlier. At this point she was taken directly to immigration detention and removed two weeks later. Nyesha said she was unable to appeal the last decision because she never received the letter explaining that her latest application had been denied. By the time she was informed in her interview, and subsequently detained, the period in which she would have been allowed to appeal had elapsed. Nyesha felt she had been tricked by the Home Office and was offended they would go to such lengths to make her leave.

Women who had been returned to Jamaica for visa violations were especially shocked that they could be detained for immigration offences. As with those I spoke to in Yarl's Wood and the UK community, they felt confinement for immigration matters was an unduly harsh punishment. Brooke described her reaction vividly:

> They take me to a [police] station first and I was hysterical, I couldn't breathe because they put me in the cell I couldn't

> breathe because I was locked up and I was like, my God … what is this?

Many were unaware of the penalties of overstaying a visa. Eve was picked up by immigration after a chance encounter with the police, she had never considered there would be consequences when she overstayed:

> I never know it was like what I … It wasn't what I expected. I thought it was more … you understand I never know that you could have hassle from immigration and deportation. I never know, I just see life. I was seeking life. For myself, and my kids.

The treatment of women when first encountering immigration enforcement did little to help them understand what was happening, adding a feeling of vilification to their general sense of injustice. Malene's journey to immigration detention began with an interview at an immigration office. She remembered how the staff had taken her belongings away and physically checked her body in case she had anything else with her. They then took her to a room where she was alone with an immigration officer. Malene had initially been sponsored to be in the UK by her cousin. She remembers the officer asked her the age of her cousins' children and forgetting them in her panic:

> I couldn't remember, because I was so, that day, I was frightened about everything, it was like I was telling the man, oh yeah, I think she's 16 or something like that. I wasn't sure. I wasn't sure to be honest. So I think that was one of the thing that let them think that I was lying, yeah, because I was panicking. Because I realised that something was wrong, you know?

Following her interview, Malene was left to wait in the immigration office, still unaware she was going to be detained. Her initial interview was at 10 am but it was evening before she was taken away in a prison van. Subsequently, Malene described a long overnight journey in the van. She described her treatment as wickedness. She felt like she was being treated as a criminal and likened her experience with slavery. She was clear that this treatment made her feel vilified, like she had committed a serious offence.

Some women remained angry about their placement in a removal centre long after their removal to Jamaica. Anna had spent a little over a month in immigration detention when she was caught without a visa. She stressed she had no complaints about the staff, but she still recalled her time there in a negative way:

> To be honest, if I tell myself, if I go back anywhere else, I wouldn't want to be in that position still, because that's not nice you know. Because it's like you are in a prison actually, it's a prison! Because you are there, you can't get to go outside. You just inside every day …

The problem for Anna, as it was for others, was that she had felt treated as a criminal. In their eyes, prison was a place for bad people who had committed serious crimes and they could not reconcile their immigration offences with this image. Cassandra had spent three months in detention. She explained to me how being treated like a criminal upset her. She felt she was not treated with dignity 'fully' because her time in detention made her feel like a criminal, lowering her self-esteem.

Others in Jamaica suggested it was not just their self-esteem that was affected, their time in detention had direct physical effects. Grace explained how the stress of being locked in detention caused her to lose weight:

> I lost about ten pounds or more. I was very slim when I came home … Yeah I was very stressed. I have never been locked up before. I have never done nothing in my life to get lock up. I never thought I would do nothing to get locked up. I been on the straight and narrow all the time, so, I could get into drugs and all them things [if I wanted], but I chose to work! I didn't have my papers and it was hard for me because I didn't want to do no drugs and them thing.

On their return to Jamaica, women had limited access to healthcare. Francelle, like a number of other women in this study, was diabetic. She had spent 13 years living in the UK before she was returned back to Jamaica. While in detention she was helped by Hibiscus,[7] an NGO based in London. Hibiscus provides practical assistance to foreign national women affected by criminal and social justice issues, to send some of her possessions home, and was provided with some medication for her trip home. However, once she was in the country, she struggled to afford her medicine regularly, she explained:

> It wasn't much so since I came I went to the clinic and they do give me some [medicine], but when I go to get it here I get it free sometime, sometime I get some, sometime I don't get the rest. I have to buy them. Can't afford to buy them so I don't.

Women explained that they were sometimes able to see a doctor or go to a clinic for free, but it was irregular and they often had to go without medication, recommended medical tests, or other needs, like glasses, because they could not afford them.

Being a woman in Jamaica

Women described important aspects of their identity they were unable to maintain on their return and how this impacted on their sense of self-worth and well-being. There was a perception amongst the community most women removed to the Jamaica were returning to that if a woman has spent time overseas, they have had the opportunity to better themselves and gain wealth for themselves and their families. The expectation, if returning from abroad, was that women would return with evidence of that wealth. In addition, mothers returned to Jamaica were likely to resume their role as breadwinner for their families, also assuming the caring role of their children now they had physically returned. In many cases these demands were impossible to meet and impacted on the way women felt about themselves. There is a long history of family members emigrating from developing nations then returning with increased wealth and ample social and cultural capital to share. In turn, entire families are helped to improve their social position (Connell and Conway, 2000; Conway and Cohen, 1998). Daloris, from earlier, explained how she had circumvented the label of deportee by preparing for her departure from prison:

> When I come back you could not tell that I have been deported. Because I come with a suitcase and I was properly dressed and at the prison, I buy like shampoo, condition, soap and all these stuff so I carry those back with me as well so I would be able to give out too, so people wouldn't know if I don't tell them.

If, unlike Daloris, women were able to hide their status as a returned person and were unable to meet the expectations of wealth and to help their families reported feeling the opposite of self-confident. These women were embarrassed and lacked the self-esteem to be seen by anybody outside their home. Malene explained how she feared facing her community:

> So when I came the night, the morning when I was supposed to come outside, I was ashamed. I said to my mum, I'm not going out there. Because people know that I come home, I'm not going to face them.

It was, however, not always as simple as looking the part and although women tried to hide their immigration status to avoid the categorisation of 'deportee,' their attempts were rarely successful. Women who may have initially hidden their means of return explained that members of their community began to challenge why they had come back to Jamaica, and were then curious why they were not returning to England. Nyesha, after spending eight years in the UK before her administrative removal, explained how people began to question her, and the impact this had on her sense of dignity:

> They said, you go away for so long, why you come back here to just sit down like this, and they will question you. How much did you pay for your fare? How much did you do that and, so I know they have it in them. That I am deported. And they thinking, sometimes they say you can't even buy this here, and you been away for so long. Can you buy me this, and you don't even have money, you can't even do your hair, you can't even … you know … which is very undignified. To me. You understand?

The welcome received by family and friends on return was also influenced by women's behaviour when they were abroad, and whether they shared their perceived wealth with their family and friends during their time away. The importance of remittances made by family members who have emigrated overseas are clearly evidenced in academic literature, where they are shown to be fundamental to many households, allowing greater opportunities for development, such as schooling (Connell and Conway, 2000). Remittances also protect against income shocks caused by natural disasters, such as hurricanes, that are common in the Caribbean region (Clarke and Wallsten, 2003). The return to Jamaica, thus, resulted in the loss of a valuable source of income that many children and other family members were relying on to survive.

Remittances also had an important role to play in the reception women would receive on their return to Jamaica. Tia had spent 11 years in the UK, of which she spent most of her time caring for her mother. When her mother died, she was forced from her home by her step-sisters. She needed to find more substantial employment to cover her new living expenses, so she went to the Job Centre[8] in search of work. There, she used her passport as identification, however, this led to the discovery that her visa was fraudulent and she was removed following a six-week stay in immigration detention. Tia explained how she had been sending money back to the rest of her family in Jamaica while she was away:

> In Jamaica, they watch. You see when you take that plane and gone, if you treat your family good, they treat you when you come back good. Understand? In everything you have to treat your family first. Treat your family, if you get a dollar, you send something of the dollar for them, and that's how comes I can survive.

In return for her relative generosity, Tia now survived with some help from friends. Despite her best efforts, though, she was still struggling to find enough money to eat and house herself.

Another dimension of returning to Jamaica as a woman was that they were expected to 'look' a certain way that reflected the perceived wealth from their time oversees. Joanne explained how she was expected to look like she had travelled. She was taken to immigration detention when she wanted to sign on and was returned to Jamaica with only the items she wore to the immigration office:

> I just come in and they don't look, I don't look like a woman who have travelled, because I'm going to sign on. I just look like a normal. Jeans, jacket. Brown jeans, brown shoes and a brown jacket. I don't come to Jamaica with a change of clothes or anything.

Nyesha explained how her arrival home without adequate or appropriate clothing led her to hide from her community:

> When I came, I didn't come out my house for month, that's even worse. Because I didn't have anything to wear, put on. For

> somebody who has been away so long, you need to look a certain way. I mean, I didn't have anything at home to put on.

Nyesha felt shamed when she was unable to fulfil the role expected of her as a woman who had worked overseas. On return, Nyesha was forced to return to the home of her former partner, although they were no longer in a relationship. Nyesha spent most of her time indoors and had little contact with anyone outside her immediate family.

Women had often relied on the help of friends and families to get by before their trip to the UK, but found this avenue of support closed to them soon after return. Naomi had spent approximately three years in prison in England. She had been struggling to earn money and was approached with an offer to carry drugs. Naomi also told me she was unaware what the packages she was asked to swallow contained. On her return from Britain in 2003, Naomi described how former friends treated her differently, no longer offering the help they once did. She described making telephone calls to former friends when in search of something for her dinner:

> I was calling a gentleman to ask him for two cabbage to steam for my dinner and he give somebody else his phone to answer to me. Yeah. And I know he is there. He give it to somebody else to answer.

Being ignored by people these women had called friends before their return hurt. Some participants were subject to aggressive acts by former friends. Women who had emigrated and spent long periods overseas were expected by the local community to have earned relatively high wages compared with their Jamaican counterparts. Those in this study were accused of wasting their opportunity, and consequently they received less help from their community to resettle in Jamaica. Anna, who had been in the UK for two years before she was held by immigration in 2005, described how she isolated herself on return to avoid hard questioning about her situation:

> They say oooh you up foreign and you come back in here, they want me to get them something, give them that. So I just stay to myself. If they going to ask me for something that is what they is going to say after. [They asked me] was there wasting your time, why did you overstay in the first place?

Women were embarrassed. They isolated themselves to avoid the harsh judgements of those in their communities in a bid to escape the emotional consequences of their treatment by others. However, in doing so they often suffered from further social isolation and the depression that often come alongside it, such as those experienced by men and women in Turnbull's (2017) work.

Nyesha and Joanne's returns to Jamaica without appropriate clothing was a direct result of immigration detention policy, where women and men can be detained suddenly and with no ability to collect up their possessions to return them to Jamaica. Turnbull (2017) described a similar lack of possessions among those returned from detention in her work. Turnbull writes that the sudden removal of men and women from detention stopped them preparing what would help them to (re-) integrate on arrival. Sudden detention does not allow people time to sell possessions, withdraw funds from bank accounts, or collect items such as valuable electronics or certificates of achievement required for employment. In Turnbull's work this inability to prepare is linked with feelings of indignity and injustice, where men and women feel they are being disproportionally punished (Turnbull, 2017). People felt humiliated by their return when they had nothing to show from their time in the UK, and the punitive nature of this practice stayed with men and women once they had been removed (Turnbull, 2017). The loss of personal effects and the means to help themselves and their families on return was felt by the women in this study to be an especially unjust and unfair punishment.

In some cases, women were forced to leave behind the entire contents of their homes in the UK. Malene explained the confusion surrounding her departure from the UK after 11 years there:

> I don't know what was really, happening, I don't know what … I don't know what is really happening. Then they saying that they going to they bought a ticket for me, an airline ticket. So they just force me out, force me. That's it. I didn't get my clothes, I didn't get nothing.

When asked where her clothes were, Malene replied: 'They were at the house. I lost everything. I lost everything.' This loss was especially painful for Malene, and others, because she knew the value of her possessions in Jamaica. She explained how she could have sold clothes or other possessions on her return and make some money from them.

Some women were helped by friends, or Hibiscus, to put together a suitcase for their return home, or to send clothing and other items to Jamaica for them. This was an immense help for women, at least initially. As Daloris explained earlier, she was helped by the fact that she had been in prison. This allowed her to prepare for her return. She also explained that her close friends who knew she had been in prison had helped keep up the story that she had just returned from travelling. Seanna had four children when she accepted the offer to take drugs to the UK, the father of her children had died when her youngest child was two years old, and at the time the smugglers offered her the chance to carry drugs to the UK they were living in a kitchen. She believed taking drugs to the UK was the best chance for a better life for her children. She too, explained how her time in prison had helped her prepare for her return to Jamaica. She told me how, in the month leading up to her release date, friends she had in the UK brought her suitcases with clothes in. She also worked while in prison and was able to send money back to her family in Jamaica. Seanna was excited to return home, she explained how she had also attended school while in prison, bettering her chances at home by having an education. She explained that she had her first child at 14, and so she missed out on the opportunity to continue her schooling. So, when the time came for her to leave prison, via immigration detention, she was well prepared:

> Officers prepared us, other what things sent in that were needed for Jamaica and, everything was ready for me to go to the detention centre so when I got the paper bought whether I want to stay in the UK or whatever, and then when I reach the detention centre, that paper I tore it up. Because I didn't want to fight, there is nothing to fight about you know. I just wanted to come home to my children.

Like Seanna, many women were excited to come home and be with their children again. However, reunification with children was not typically straightforward. Women had often spent many years away. On return, relationships could be tense. Malene described the interactions she had with her daughter, who was close to turning 18:

> She keep arguing with me. I don't know you, you is not my mum, you know? And I'm saying to her, I used to help you when I was

> over there … But it is like I can't talk to her. When I'm saying something, she don't want to listen to me. She's telling me, it's like she's carrying a hatred for me.

Nyesha felt her son resented her absence during his childhood and described her struggles to build back their relationship:

> I tell you, my youngest son he resent me so much. I don't know if it is because I left him so young, he been in touch, but until now I still can't build, (cries) I can't build back that relationship. Sometimes I think I would be better off, I would be better off if I didn't leave.

Women often described how they had left Jamaica in the first instance, for their offspring. Their role as providers for their children was of exceptional importance. I asked Eve how she felt when she lived in London and could provide for her children:

> Good. Independent. Proud. Yeah man, you feel like you do something to survive … Yeah man, you feel … it's not much but you feel rich. Trust me, feel like saying you independent, you're able, to make something, cause my son, call and he hungry, me can make it happen, you understand.

It is common in Jamaica for mothers to emigrate in order to make a better life for their children. However, academic research has shown there can be negative consequences for children left behind (Crawford-Brown, 1999; Dillon and Walsh, 2012; Pottinger, 2005). These include poor school attendance, psychological problems (Pottinger, 2005), and health and emotional problems (Dillon and Walsh, 2012). In addition, the absence of a mother to emigration was shown by Crawford-Brown to increase the likelihood that boys would become involved in criminal behaviour (Crawford-Brown, 1999). Mothers take a risk when they emigrate away from their families in search of work. If they are then returned home with little to show for their time away, they must also reconcile themselves with the knowledge that their children may have suffered with little recompense. This was distressing for mothers.

Many women could not always afford to feed their children. Women described how they had to choose between feeding their offspring or sending them to school. Shantel had spent nine months in prison in the

UK for carrying drugs. She had accepted the drugs with the idea to stay in the UK after and send back money for the two children she had at the time, the youngest of which was a baby. Since return Shantel has given birth to three more children, and described to me why she felt unable to send them to school:

> You have to have lunch money for them, cause you can't send them with empty stomach. It's better that they outside and they hustle a bit and get some dumpling and butter, then they go to school. But, you understand. When you send them [to school] … they not taking in the lesson because its too much empty in the stomach.

Women were aware of the importance of education for the future of their children and their inability to send them to school upset them. Many had limited education themselves and wanted a better future for their children. Their failure to provide food and schooling for their children made them feel guilty and ashamed.

In what is an otherwise dire portrait of women and dignity in Jamaica, there were some exceptions. Women who had spent time in prison in the UK benefited from the ability to gain an education and this added to their sense of self-esteem and worth. Similarly, women who were able to prepare for their return to Jamaica were better placed to offset the impact of violations to dignity.

As mentioned above, those who were deported for criminal offences and those who were removed due to administrative migration offences had different experiences on return. One factor that led to this difference was education. Women often had limited education on arrival to the UK. Those who had spent time in prison had benefited from the education provided in them. This group of women improved their English and maths skills and attended courses on life skills and decision-making. Some told me with pride about the courses they undertook while in prison. Seanna, who had left school at 14 when she fell pregnant with her first child, was bursting with excitement when she recalled the courses she attended in prison:

> Computer, social and life skills, I do maths, English, I did a teaching course. I did a gym course, in netball and basketball, to be a coach and I work as well in craft shop, making post card and all of that. I did all, history test, I passed the history test and exam, with all honours!

Not all former prisoners undertook the mass of courses recounted by Seanna, but even a basic education was useful. Daloris had spent three years in prison in England before she returned in 2001. She was 21 and described herself as a party girl when she accepted the offer to carry drugs to the UK. She had a five-year-old son at the time. While Daloris was in prison she focused purely on her reading and writing. I asked her if the skills she had learned from the courses had been helpful since she had come home:

> Yes, because before I went there I drop out of school very early … but going there for 3 and a half years came down reading and all of them things there, teach me and I come back home now, it's good.

Many of the participants in the study emphasised the importance of learning to read and write. Most jobs required numeracy and writing skills as a minimum, and those women who were unable to fulfil this criterion found their employment opportunities further restricted.

The education gained in prison did not, unfortunately, ensure employment on return to Jamaica. However, it did seem to help women with their self-esteem. Olivia, who was introduced earlier, stressed the usefulness of life skills when I asked if her education in prison had been helpful on return:

> Yeah, me a better person, me a better person. And I used to be very ignorant and those things, cause I went into even this, um, this seminar, like seminar for awareness. Yeah.

Some also discussed how they had used their new-found skills to encourage others to better their situation. Seanna had spent four years in prison for carrying drugs. Since her return she had become involved helping other women and men returned to Jamaica:

> Um, most, you know what I implement the most? Anger management. I did a course because I was a very angry person, and I have implemented that, and oh I did a course called enhanced thinking skills, and this is what changed my life forever now, to this person that I can um, mentor others and motivate others.

The contribution Seanna was able to make to her community gave her a sense of worth and purpose that most women in this study were unable to find.

Just as they appreciated the education in prison, women who had been incarcerated for a criminal act also benefited from the more established system to help them prepare for their release from prison and return. The help they received typically came from services provided by Hibiscus. Yasmin had been forced to carry drugs to the UK was intercepted on arrival and spent four years in prison in the UK. She described the practical and emotional benefits of help provided by a member of the Hibiscus team:

> [A woman from Hibiscus] come and talk to us, if you have no one in the UK to offer us anything or tell our problem … she send some clothes for us or whatever, yeah, when we are going home. Anyone foreign national she will send some things for them to wear home.

Hibiscus was the only NGO women regularly referenced during interviews, and mostly in the context of prison. Hibiscus are present in some UK detention centres, however, many women I spoke with were not aware of their detention-based service. When I interviewed women still in immigration detention, one of the barriers to preparation for removal was their perpetual hope for a last-minute injunction. These interventions meant people were unwilling or unable to accept they would genuinely be removed from the UK and therefore were reluctant to engage with Hibiscus or other services.

There were, however, some positive examples of help gleaned from Hibiscus in removal centres. Earlene, introduced earlier was made aware of Hibiscus through a friend she had made in the removal centre. They offered her £100 in cash, or to pay for an additional suitcase to take more of her belongings home. She chose the additional suitcase of belongings.

Women in detention were also likely to have spent any savings they had accrued, or used up the goodwill of friends and family to hire lawyers in order to resist their removal. This means that nothing is left for them when they return. Women are sometimes able to work in immigration detention centres; however, the roles available are limited and payment is as low as £1 per hour[9] (Bosworth, 2008, 2014). Prisoners, however, were able to work during their time in prison and could return with a small amount of savings. As exemplified earlier in this chapter, the appearance of women on return to Jamaica was an important factor in their ability to effectively resettle and protect their sense of identity and self-esteem. The ability to save towards this, is thus an important protective factor against violations to their sense of dignity on return.

Conclusion

Women returned to Jamaica wanted to be treated fairly, justly, and with respect for their personal circumstances. Instead, they experienced persistent violations to their dignity across all spheres of their lives; women were labelled and stigmatised when they returned to Jamaica, they were considered 'criminal' and treated as such. Many discovered that their previous circle of friends and family were much less willing to offer their support than they had expected and hoped. Women found it challenging to look respectable, support their children, or gain employment, and as a consequence, their sense of self-worth suffered. Some had also been deeply offended by the treatment they received from the UK government during the process of their removal. Combining all these aspects, they described to me a set of circumstances in which it was difficult, if not impossible, to maintain their sense of self-worth. In their testimonies, a set of overarching themes emerge which can be related to the concept of dignity. These factors include ones that were present in detention and in the community – of being labelled, criminalised, and vilified.

These kinds of complaints surrounding injustice in the detention and removal system of the UK are common throughout this book; yet they were more pronounced in Jamaica where they contrasted significantly with the interviews of women who had spent time in prison and then removed shortly after. This group of women did not appear to suffer the indignity of unjust treatment. Instead, they saw detention as part of their transition to going home, and importantly, going home was their desire. This finding suggests the absence of legitimacy may be a factor in women's perception of dignified treatment. Bosworth has delved into the question of whether immigration removal centres can be legitimate, arguing that these spaces present a substantial deficit of legitimacy (Bosworth, 2013). As institutions that hold men and women indefinitely and lack judicial oversight, it is hard to disagree (Bosworth, 2013; Bosworth and Turnbull, 2015).

The differences between those who had migrated to the UK for work or school and others who travelled with drugs were also important. Their experiences on return were heavily influenced by their reasons for leaving. Some of the variance can be easily explained, such as the fact that those who had been in prison had never spent time in the country outside these institutions. Most women in this group had never expected to stay in the UK, and were happy to return to Jamaica as soon as possible. Alternatively, those who had lived in the UK community often fought their removal to Jamaica. If someone had lived in the community, they had often become part of it; many had family and friends there and few connections left in Jamaica. On return the women from each group faced different challenges as they tried to negotiate a life for themselves.

Acknowledgement

Gerlach, A. (2018) 'Helping women prepare for removal: The case of Jamaica,' in *After Deportation: Ethnographic Perspectives*, edited by Shahram Khosravi. London: Palgrave Macmillan, ISBN 978-3-319-57267-3. Parts of this work have been reproduced in this chapter with permission of Palgrave Macmillan.

Notes

1 Jocelyn was not clear on what 'helping' involved, but referenced how she loved to help people, and this is how she came to be in trouble.
2 Participants were unclear what their 'national record' contained, but most likely they were referring to police records held by the Ministry of National Security.
3 It was unclear if this was fact or rumour, though it was brought up by almost all women interviewed.
4 The female unemployment rate has since fallen to 14.1 per cent, as reported in October 2017 (Statistics Institute of Jamaica, 2018).
5 For a detailed historical overview of women working in the informal urban economy of Kingston, Jamaica, see Harrison (1988).
6 HM Revenue and Customs is the government department in the UK responsible for collecting taxes.
7 See http://hibiscusinitiatives.org.uk/ for full details.
8 In the UK, the 'Job Centre' is where individuals go to seek employment and/or support from the government if they are unemployed.
9 The issue of pay in immigration detention was recently the subject of a judicial review, with ten people formerly held in removal centres challenging the practice (see Bales and Mayblin, 2017).

References

Bailey C (2013) Exploring female motivations for drug smuggling on the island of Barbados: Evidence from her majesty's prison, Barbados. *Feminist Criminology* 8(2): 117–141. https://doi.org/10.1177/1557085112474837.

Bales K and Mayblin L (2017) *'Paid work' or Underpaid Labour? The Labour Exploitation of Detainees within Immigration Detention.* Bristol: Bristol University. Available at: https://legalresearch.blogs.bris.ac.uk/2017/09/paid-work-or-underpaid-labour-the-labour-exploitation-of-detainees-within-immigration-detention/.

Batnitzky A and McDowell L (2011) Migration, nursing, institutional discrimination and emotional/affective labour: Ethnicity and labour stratification in the UK national health service. *Social and Cultural Geography* 12(2): 181–201. https://doi.org/10.1080/14649365.2011.545142.

Blank L (2007) *Situation Analysis of Children and Women in the Eastern Caribbean.* Barbados: UNICEF.

Bosworth M (2008) Immigration detention. *Criminal Justice Matters* 71(1): 24–25. https://doi.org/10.1080/09627250801937611.

Bosworth M (2013) Can Immigration Detention Centres Be legitimate? Understanding confinement in a global world. In: Bosworth M and Aas K (eds.) *The Borders of Punishment Migration, Citizenship, and Social Exclusion.* Oxford: Oxford University Press, pp. 149–165

Bosworth M (2014) *Inside Immigration Detention.* Oxford: Oxford University Press.

Bosworth M and Turnbull S (2015) Immigration detention and the expansion of penal power in the UK. In: Reiter K and Koenig A (eds.) *Extreme Punishment.* London: Palgrave, pp. 50–67.

Brown D (1997) Workforce losses and return migration to the Caribbean: A case study of Jamaican nurses. In: Pessar P (ed.) *Caribbean Circuits: New Directions in the Study of Caribbean Migration.* New York: Centre for Migration Studies.

Campbell H (2008) Female drug smugglers on the U.S.-Mexico border: Gender, crime, and empowerment. *Anthropological Quarterly* 81(1): 233–267.

Clarke C (2006) Politics, violence and drugs in Kingston, Jamaica. *Bulletin of Latin American Research* 25(3): 420–440. https://doi.org/10.1111/j.0261-3050.2006.00205.x.

Clarke G and Wallsten S (2003) Do remittances act like insurance? Evidence from a natural disaster in Jamaica. *SSRN Electronic Journal* 202. https://doi.org/10.2139/ssrn.373480.

Connell J and Conway D (2000) Migration and remittances in island microstates: A Comparative perspective on the South Pacific and the Caribbean. *International Journal of Urban and Regional Research* 24(1): 52–78. https://doi.org/10.1111/1468-2427.00235.

Conway D and Cohen J (1998) Consequences of migration and remittances for Mexican transnational communities. *Economic Geography* 74(1): 26–44.

Crawford-Brown C (1999) *Who Will Save Our Children? The Plight of the Jamaican Child in the 1990's.* Kingston, Jamaica: Canoe Press, University of the West Indies.

Dillon M and Walsh C (2012) Left behind: The experiences of children of the Caribbean whose parents have migrated. *Journal of Comparative Family Studies* 43(6): 871–902.

Esmee Fairbairn Foundation (2003) *A Bitter Pill to Swallow: The Sentencing of Foreign National Drug Couriers*. London: Esmee Fairbairn Foundation.

Foner N (1985) Race and color: Jamaican migrants in London and New York City. *The International Migration Review* 19(4): 708–727. https://doi.org/10.2307/2546105.

Golash-Boza T (2015) *Deported: Immigration Policing, Disposable Labour, and Global Capitalism*. New York and London: New York University Press.

Harrison F (1988) Women in Jamaica's urban informal economy: Insights from a Kingston slum. *New West Indian Guide* 62(3/4): 103–128. https://doi.org/10.1163/13822373-90002040.

Headley B (2006) Giving critical context to the deportee phenomenon of blame. *Social Justice* 33(1): 40–56.

Klein A, Day M and Harriot A (2004) *Caribbean Drugs: From Criminalization to Harm Reduction*. New York: Zed Books.

Miller A (2012) Deportation as a process of irreversible transformation. *Journal of Ethnic and Migration Studies* 38(May): 131–146. https://doi.org/10.1080/1369183X.2012.640024.

Mujtaba B, Cavico F, Hinds RM, et al. (2006) Age discrimination in the workplace: Cultural paradigms associated with age in Afghanistan, Jamaica, Turkey, and the United States. *The Journal of Applied Management and Entrepreneurship* 11(1): 17.

Mujtaba BG, Hinds RM and Oskal C (2004) Cultural perspectives on aging and older individuals. *Journal of Business* 2(12): 31–44.

Pottinger AM (2005) Children's experience of loss by parental migration in inner-city Jamaica. *The American Journal of Orthopsychiatry* 75(4): 485–496. https://doi.org/10.1037/0002-9432.75.4.485.

Statistics Institute of Jamaica. (2016). *Unemployment Rates by Age Group*. Kingston, Jamaica: Labour Force Statistics.http://statinja.gov.jm/LabourForce/NewLFS.aspx

Thomas-Hope EM (2002) *Explanation in Caribbean Migration: Perception and the Image: Jamaica, Barbados, St. Vincent*. 2nd ed. London: Macmillan.

Tidrick G (1966) Some aspects of Jamaican emigration to the United Kingdom 1953–1962. *Social and Economic Studies* 15(1): 22–39.

Turnbull S (2017) Starting again: Life after deportation from the UK. In: Khosravi S (ed.) *After Deportation: Ethnographic Perspectives*. London: Palgrave Macmillan, pp. 37–62.

5
INDIGNITY

At the outset of this book, I presented an overview of 'dignity' as a concept that is vague and difficult to conceptualise in any meaningful way. But this does not mean it is not impossible, nor that we should not try to do so. The findings offered in this book support the notion that dignity is important to women who have spent time in immigration detention and that the way in which their dignity is, or is not, respected within detention and after release or removal has a lasting impact. Below, I attempt to define dignity using their words, and illustrate how the concept was repeatedly violated as a result of their time in, and after, detention.

Defining the experience of dignity

When asked to define dignity, women who participated in this research were easily able to offer some explanation as to what the concept entailed. Defining dignity was posed to participants at the natural end of discussions surrounding their current situation, be that in detention, the UK community, or living in Jamaica. The purpose of this was to avoid influencing their testimony, allowing for responses that were as subjective as possible before asking them to delve into dignity. In a number of cases the term had arisen naturally throughout the conversation, providing further evidence for the importance of the concept to the women involved. The discussions varied substantially, as expected; however, there were three prominent descriptions that were frequent throughout: Dignity as an action, dignity as a possession, and dignity as a state of being.

DOI: 10.4324/9780367823153-6

Dignity as an action

Dignity as an action, is the way in which someone is made, or requested, to perform an act. A violation to dignity in this context was described by women as forcing another individual into a situation, or setting them a task, that you would not be willing to do or be in yourself. A vivid example came from Abigay who utilised her Christian faith to help explain the concept to me. I met Abigay in immigration detention, she was from Jamaica and fighting her removal there because she feared she would be attacked by gangs if she was to return. Like most women in detention, our interview was held in Abigay's room. On the desk in Abigay's room she had a carton of juice she had earlier purchased from the on-site shop. She used this to explain dignity to me. As Abigay picked up the carton of juice, she explained that if the carton of juice was too heavy for her to pick up, she would not expect me to pick up the carton. Much like the biblical 'do unto others what you would have done unto you,' to not respect dignity in this way was to make a person undertake an act that you would not perform yourself. Edwina, who I interviewed in Jamaica, described it in a similar way, she told me that dignity was respect, and respect was shown through manners: 'With manners. You pass someone with "hi, good morning." Good evening. yeah. That is manners.' For Edwina, these simple human interactions with other people illustrated dignity as an action.

This definition of dignity is reflected in many of the worst examples of violations to dignity, such as the work from Stoecker (2011) where he discussed the menial labours forced on the Jewish community during the Holocaust, such as forcing them to scrub pavements. In this example, it is not the act of scrubbing pavements, but the way in which Jewish people were forced to scrub pavements, an act that Nazi's would never force each other to endure. Likewise, in a more recent account of dignity framing, Halliday and Liu (2021) describe the way in which poor farming communities in China have been stripped of their properties in order for the government to profit from tourism. The lack of dignity here is not the removal of property or land, but the way in which people who protested the removal were forced into 're-education' labour camps. This is not an act that would be forced upon the ruling elite.

For the women in this study, dignity as an action was violated in many different ways. In immigration detention, the very act of depriving someone of their liberty was an offence to their dignity. When I asked Barbara, a citizen of the USA, who I met in detention, if she felt dignity in detention was possible, she replied:

> No. When you house people like cattle in a locked building, with locked doors there is no dignity there. That's meant for people who break the law, and knew they were breaking the law and did it anyway.

Adding to this, Maria explained that there was little that could be done to dispel the 'wrong' feeling that came with being held in immigration detention, when asked if she felt she was treated with dignity, she told me:

> No, I don't feel that. I don't feel that they have … a social ability to make you feel comfortable in here. Even though they have tried their best, doing the hairdressing salon, doing the library, doing certain things. But it still doesn't feel right to be detained.

The quotes from Barbara and Maria here illustrate the underlying feeling of being wronged that was felt by many women in detention. It was, fundamentally, the act of detaining women in detention that caused them to feel their dignity was violated, and little could be done to dispel this feeling.

Dignity as a possession

Dignity was described by other women as a kind of possession. It was an item that a person must hold on to in order to keep it, and notably, it was possible for others to take dignity, as a possession, away. Eve, who I met in Jamaica, had lived in the UK for four years before she was returned there. She had overstayed her visitor visa and was taken to detention after a chance encounter with the police where she was unable to provide evidence of her right to stay in the UK. She described dignity in such terms: 'Your dignity is something that you hold onto, you understand? Your dignity is something you want die with. You understand? You don't want somebody to take that from you.' Eve expressed this definition in the context of her struggles to earn enough money from a makeshift shop on the street in Jamaica to feed her children. She felt that her dignity was something she had to constantly fight for, in order to maintain it. In the case of Eve, and many others, she felt that holding on to her dignity was the difference between living a worthy life or a shameful one. Cassandra, who also spoke to me from Jamaica, was removed to the country after a failed asylum application. She provided a practical illustration of how this dignity as a possession was violated on her removal flight. She, along with another Jamaican woman, had been handcuffed when being seated on the plane, which was a commercial flight to Jamaica with other passengers:

> It make us, our dignity, because knowing that other passengers were on the plane as well. I know they take away our dignity, our pride as well because we were ashamed. Because they handcuff us. Yeah.

Cassandra demonstrates here the way in which an action performed by others very clearly 'takes away' her dignity, as though it was an object or a shield that had been removed.

Dignity as a state of being

Others reflected on dignity as a state of being. Dignity was the way in which an individual held themselves. Audree had come to the UK to study, but was returned to Jamaica after two years when it was discovered she had overstayed her visa, she described dignity as a state of being, or a feeling: 'Maybe your pride? Your pride and everything about yourself actually. Your pride, how you carry yourself. How you look about yourself and everything.' Reflecting on dignity in this way, women presented the image of a strong woman. She stands straight and tall, her shoulder braced as though fighting the wind, her head held high, an image of dignity, as described here by Cleona, who I met in Jamaica: 'Well, dignity, I turn to myself, for my dignity I want to put myself, put my shoulder to the wind, lift up my head and certain things that I want to go out for, work, help meself.' This picture was the ideal, and women compared themselves to this. Lack of dignity, in the alternative, was presented as a woman cowering, she holds her head low, making herself as small and unassuming as possible.

The explanations and descriptions of dignity shared by the women in this study were varied and nuanced, and sometimes contradictory, but they all link to the idea that dignity is a person's belief that they are worth something. As an action, the belief in self-worth is that they are being forced into a situation or behaviour that they believe is below them. As a possession, when removed, part of the self is removed alongside their dignity which results in the value of the person to be lessened. Finally, as a state of being, dignity is embodied by the individual, and the person they feel they are can be visualised as somewhere between the woman standing strong, or the alternative image of a woman, cowering and fearful of the world. In the following paragraphs, the stories of women in detention, and after, illustrate how acts which impact on dignity are experienced as painful, and how immigration enforcement ultimately chips away at women's dignity.

Key themes of dignity in immigration detention and after

The examples of dignity violations in immigration detention and after were many, and diverse. Yet, there were three key themes that were consistent throughout most of the women's experience: Vilification, lack of autonomy, and 'diminishment.' In relation to women's descriptions of the concept of dignity, the conditions of detention clearly offended their sense of dignity through forcing them into actions that felt undignified, in a way that made it difficult for women to hold onto their sense of self-worth. As a result, the indignity caused by these violations led to a collection of women who were greatly distressed by their detention. In the following paragraphs, the experience of detention is expressed through these three key themes.

Vilification

Vilification is to be made to feel as though you are in some way 'bad,' or morally inferior. For women in detention, the violation to their dignity arose from the disconnect between their own perceived sense of being a 'good' person and their treatment at the hands of the Home Office. It is well documented in detention literature that detention centres have the look, and feel, of prisons (Bosworth, 2014, 2017; Bosworth et al., 2016), and the buildings are, in some cases, former prison buildings. Yarl's Wood, the detention centre where this research was based, have made efforts to soften the environment for the women held there, including paintings on the walls, a craft room, and the addition of a hair salon, for example. However, the centre is still unmistakably carceral, with high walls, barred windows, tall fences, and gates surrounding the buildings. These attributes overwhelm any softening measures put in place in the centre. When I asked Samantha, who had been in detention for almost a year following a prison sentence, to explain to me in what way Yarl's Wood looked and felt like a prison, she laughed at me, and pointed out the window of her room to the barbed wire, high walls, and gates we could both see. She, and others, found the proposal that Yarl's Wood was not a prison offensive.

The prison like environment implied to women that they were dangerous, that they were not safe to be in the community, and ultimately, the country. Luciana, who I met in detention, described how this made her feel:

> They really really, they make us feel like we are dangerous people, they feel afraid of us. Look at me! I have never done nothing wrong. I feel as … yes, I don't have papers. But you know, and they made me feel like they lock me, and they make sure I am lock and they look at me like, ok, you have to stay there. Because you … morally … I don't know what they are thinking, but they make me feel really bad.

To women who had not committed a criminal offence, to be treated as though they were criminal was hurtful, because it was in direct opposition to their sense of self as an upstanding moral citizen. I met Wendy when she was in detention, she was facing removal to Jamaica after it was established that she had overstayed her visa. She had a son and four grandchildren in the UK and she was fighting to stay to be with them, her partner had died many years ago and her UK family were the only family she had. Wendy described to me how being taken to detention impacted her sense of dignity:

> for the main fact that they bring you in here, I think my dignity gone. You know why I say that? I wasn't looking to be in a place like this. My grandkids know that their grandmother in detention for nothing! You know, detained for nothing, you know.

Wendy could not comprehend the idea of a grandmother locked up in a removal centre as it was so far removed from her sense of identity as a caring and maternal figure.

Many women explained to me how they volunteered with charity organisations in their community, attended church regularly, or looked after the children of their friends and family to help out. Maria had lived in the UK for four and a half years; she had a British husband and a two-year-old daughter who would be left behind if she was removed. She spent much of our interview telling me of her good character, she used the example of a community garden she had helped to develop in her street, and how she was on good terms with all her neighbours:

> where I lived for the last four and a half years, we even have, we made our streets look so pretty. We live up on ★★★★[1] and what we have done in four and a half years we have made our streets look so pretty, we've made flower boxes like the group of people who have made flower boxes and we make all the gardens around ★★★★ pretty.

Maria's confidence was suffering from the label of criminal as a result of detention, and she told me she was becoming increasingly confused and nervous, as she was constantly trying to prove she was not a bad person. Maria went on to describe how her incarceration, having committed no criminal act, felt painful:

> Imagine, you have your family. (laughs ironically). But it make you feel here … you know you didn't steal (starts to cry), you didn't do nothing wrong to no-one. That's what make you feel really bad you know. We have a family, I have a baby. Yesterday she was four years.

Like Maria, many women felt that being in a prison was hurtful and that their incarceration felt like a blow to their sense of self as a good moral person. The women could not understand what they had done wrong to deserve such treatment, and felt imprisonment was not a justifiable response to their administrative errors or transgressions in relation to their immigration status.

Women who had been in prison before their stay in immigration detention too felt their imprisonment there was unjust and felt vilified by it. For this population, the offence hinged on the indefinite nature of immigration detention. Most women in this group confessed relatively minor criminal offences such as fraud, shop lifting, or a fight that led to a prison sentence, yet they said, they were suffering the harsh punishment of much 'worse' offenders, such as 'rapists,' 'murderers,' and 'terrorists.' Chrissie, who I met in detention, reflected on the relative punishment of detention, by rightly, comparing the difference of time incarcerated to that of people who have committed serious crimes: 'This is a country, they encourage people, even if I was John Jihad, terrorist, I would be out on bail.' 'Jihadi John' is a colloquial name given to a member of extremist group ISIL who conducted a series of beheadings. He was a member of a four-person terrorist cell, all of which had English accents and had been dubbed 'The Beatles,' the assumption being that 'John' was given as a nickname to reflect John Lennon, the singer of the band. Since he became a figure in popular media around 2014–15, Jihadi John has been held up as a symbol of the 'worst' possible type of terrorist, exactly because his British accent, and eventual discovery that he was a university educated man of British nationality, culturally, situated him as someone who had turned on his country (Malcolm, 2016). It is notable, then, that Chrissie had chosen Jihadi John in her example. She considered her treatment worse than that which would be considered for an especially notorious criminal of the UK.

The 'life sentence' of indefinite detention was also a significant factor in the vilification of women. In prison, they told me, they at least had a release date to work towards, and this gave them a sense of purpose and trajectory in time. In detention, where their incarceration is potentially endless, they did not have this crutch to help ease their pains of imprisonment. They felt this was undeserved, and that they too were vilified much more than their sense of identity allowed. Regina, had previously been in prison, and told me of how she preferred it to immigration detention:

> I like in prison you know, because you know the day you go out. Because they give you paper when you come in supposed to come to you within one week. You sentence is so so many days, but you do so so so and so so so, so you released then and then. Done. Ok. And you are sitting and waiting every day. That's what you do in there. And here? At the moment I feel like I'm doing a life sentence. You know, nearly life, already seven months done. (laughs ironically)

This preference for prison over detention was repeated by many women in the study, not only due to the tangibility of a release date but also the clear rules and regulations there that they felt were lacking in the removal centre.

Lack of autonomy

Autonomy refers to an ability to direct your own life (Dupré, 2009). Lack of autonomy, in contrast, suggests an individual is somehow constrained by another person, or institution, in their ability to make decisions. In literature on health, an ability to direct your own life is a key determinant of dignified treatment (Griffiths, 2013; Jacobson, 2009; Nussbaum, 1997; Phelps, 2009), and the lack of this in detention was fundamental to the experience of women incarcerated there. The purpose of immigration detention is to hold individuals in a space that ensures they are available for return to their country of birth. There is an obvious lack of autonomy in the very nature of the institution of detention in this sense; however, the offence to dignity here is not the restriction of detention, per se, but rather the combination of indefinite detention and unnecessary and unfair restrictions that are due to the detention.

Immigration detention in the UK remains indefinite, an individual can never know if or when they will be released (or removed) from their imprisonment. This 'indefinite sentence' was seen as overtly punitive to the women and it led to the feeling of vilification in the population. But indefinite detention has another consequence, in that this practice inherently stops an individual from the ability to plan for their future, in the event of either outcome of release or removal. Vicky, who had been detained following a prison sentence, had been in the UK since she was a child, and spoke with a thick South London accent while explaining her frustration at the way her case was managed:

> Look at me! with my sentence, and with the immigration matters, it's over two years now and now you lot just decide to give me deportation decision and order all at once. Hold that. The decision should have come a year ago. Then I've got a year to fight whatever so they can make an order or not. Guess what, it's your lucky day you're getting it both at once. How do you work that one out? Who's made this decision? Who is my case worker? I've never seen them in my life, and every couple of months they change.

It is notoriously difficult for individuals to fight their immigration case from immigration detention. In a review of casework in detention HM Inspectorate of Prisons (HMIP) and the Independent Inspector of Border and Immigration (ICIBI) showed access to lawyers while in detention was limited, and the service provided poor (HMIP and ICIBI, 2012). Existing academic work also illustrates the struggle faced by men and women to access good legal representation (Bosworth, 2014; Griffiths, 2013) and also the barriers detention created in gaining access to appropriate documentation that had been left in the community, such as evidence to support an asylum claim (BID, 2009; Griffiths, 2013). Further, case workers, who are the individuals that make the decision on whether to remove an individual, are rarely accessible to people in detention. These barriers were experienced by women in detention as an affront to dignity, as they felt their detention was inherently unfair and the system disadvantaged them markedly. Luciana, while in detention, expressed to me the confusion she felt when trying to plan and organise her case:

> There are a lot of people don't know what is going to happen. No-body know. That is the problem, nobody know what is going on. Is no-one to come tell us. Oh, look that day you going to have this, or one day you gonna, you have to do this. We have to be looking, oh what I need to send, oh I need to … even sometimes we say we don't know what we are doing but we do it. They no-one, to tell us.

The confusion expressed here by Luciana is indicative of an inability to have autonomy when in detention. The indefinite nature of the incarceration, combined with processes women found almost impossible to navigate left them feeling hopeless and helpless.

Diminishment

Diminishment is when an individual is made to feel smaller through the interaction they have with another person or institution (Jacobson, 2009). As described above, women in detention struggled to access case workers and lawyers to fight their case, resulting in a lack of autonomy. This was then confounded by a perceived lack of concern regarding their complaints regarding access, and to the women, the Home Office were not concerned of their individual needs or circumstances in relation to their immigration case. This led women to feel they were unimportant to the Home Office, often describing a feeling that they had been forgotten or that they were being ignored. Anam had been a student in the UK and was being detained before she was to be returned to her home country after the English testing centre she had used for her visa had been found to be fraudulently passing applicants. In perfect English she described how she felt ignored by the Home Office after multiple attempts to prove her English test results were legitimate:

> It's really painful, to be really honest. That you are trying to convince someone that please, we are not telling that right or wrong. Just give us a chance to prove ourselves. But Home Office not wanting to give a single chance to us. I don't know why they believe in all wrong things, why they not believing all the good things?

The way in which the healthcare provision worked in detention was also a substantial factor in women's feelings of diminishment. The women I spoke with in detention complained, almost without exception, that they were suffering from a physical or mental ailment in detention. Some women had pre-existing conditions that had worsened while in detention, where others developed new problems since their imprisonment. The problems were varied but were often related to heart problems such as tightness in the chest, or irregular beating of the heart, unusual and prolonged bleeding from the bowel or uterus, headaches, and stomach problems.[2] All the women I spoke to felt neglected by the medical team on site in relation to their problems. A number had been turned away with what they felt were serious ailments and some women expressed fear that they would not get the medical help they required in an emergency. Women likened the treatment in relation to their health as less than an animal would receive in the UK, often referencing the general love of animals apparent in British society. I met Ryane in the community, she had been detained three times, though she was a victim of human trafficking. She explained various ailments in detention that went untreated, or treated improperly, and how it made her feel:

> Even the way they treat dog here, is like it is family, but the way they treated me, I fear, I was crying, I was crying all the time, I was like, what is going on? I was like, I want to go mad. You understand? It is not good, that place is not for anybody.

Women felt diminished to the point of dehumanisation, and this reference to treatment as animals, or less, was a common theme throughout. Esther described her detention as akin to chickens in a slaughterhouse:

> So … my feeling about this place is … you're like chickens (laughs), we're the chickens in (laughs), we're the chickens and all they have to do … (goes off and talks to someone who pops head in the door) … all we … all we are waiting for is which one they are going to say is to be slaughtered. That's my feeling (laughs).

When I asked Esther the impact on her, as a person, to feel like you are a chicken waiting to be slaughtered, she answered: 'The impact is devastating. The impact is absolutely … I don't know. It's heartwrenching.'

The impact of these violations to women's dignity in detention was an overwhelmingly negative picture of women in general distress. The lasting effects of detention are important to recognise as they show an immigration enforcement regime that is harmful not only at the time of incarceration but also for an indefinite time after release. Renas, who I met in the community, had fled her country fearing for her life after becoming targeted for her support of human rights. She had ambitions of doing a PhD in the UK, but found that the impact of detention had left her so unwell it was difficult to focus:

> They make my situation worse, my depression, my ability, my memory, all this affect on my body … I lost my health, my healthy, my ablility to think right way. I lost my hobby [academic work], my situation not like this. My confidence I lost, I lost my confident.

Renas was forward in telling me how this made her feel and was clear that she blamed the system of immigration enforcement and detention for her feelings:

> They like they kill us from inside. If you could [kill] you by any way this be easier, easier, cause they kill you from inside. So they are criminal, more than they kill me by knife or gun.

Renas had been free of detention for almost two years, but was still feeling the effects of her two month stay. This was common in the women who participated in interviews after being released from immigration removal centres to the community. These women's sense of dignity had been substantially wounded while in immigration detention and most were deeply hurt and unsettled by their treatment there. Women's sense of self-worth and self-esteem had plummeted since detention, as ongoing involvement with the Home Office compounded the indignity of detention. Most women I spoke with had ongoing mental health issues such as anxiety, depression, and post-traumatic stress disorder. All of the women with continuing involvement with the Home Office lived in fear of re-detention.

Fear of being returned to detention is an important focal point in the discussion of the impact of immigration detention, and it illustrates the lasting anxiety caused by incarceration there. This fear also exemplifies the continuing offence to women's dignity in the form of vilification, lack of autonomy, and diminishment. When released from immigration detention, most women were restricted by reporting conditions, where they had to attend a Home Office reporting centre regularly. The regularity of the reporting procedure was different for each woman, though usually appeared as once a week initially, extending incrementally the longer women were waiting for a decision from the Home Office in the community. Reporting to the Home Office was a focal point in the lives of the women, as people were often detained and taken to detention when reporting. Many women described increasing levels of anxiety, stress, and depressive episodes in the lead up to the day in which they were to report. I met Brenda in the community following her release, she was visibly and audibly anxious when describing her fear of re-detention:

> Whenever you be walking around, I be scared that maybe somebody is going to take me back to Yarl's Wood (change in tone of voice here – trembling). So I was all the time scared, not feel good myself knowing that any time, every month to be counted again.

The practice of reporting was described as an affront to the dignity of women as it controlled their movements and activities, thus was an offence to their autonomy. Likewise, the act of reporting is similar to that expected of ex-prisoners, who report to parole officers. Reporting was seen by the women as vilifying and they felt ashamed by the practice. Likewise, they were embarrassed by their detention, hiding the event from new friends, and families back home as the nuances between immigration detention and prison are not well understood both in the UK or abroad.

It is clear from the definitions of dignity provided by women who had experienced immigration detention, and the resulting discussions of violations to this dignity experienced in immigration removal centres, that the dignity of women in detention was not protected while the women in this study were incarcerated there. Using their definitions, the very existence of immigration removal centres is an affront to their dignity. Placing an individual in indefinite detention, in a prison like environment, fails the dignity as an action, dignity as a possession, and dignity as a state of being definitions of dignity defined by women who have experienced detention in a variety of ways.

The question then is how does dignity fit within immigration detention and in relation to women's journey after detention? In healthcare literature, autonomy, for example, is defined as the ability of an individual to control their situation within the restrictions of their medical situation, and it is generally recognised that this is possible (Gallagher and Seedhouse, 2002; Gennip et al., 2013; Henry et al., 2015; Sugarman et al., 2015). In immigration detention, however, the combination of vilification, diminishment, and loss of autonomy make dignified treatment, as defined by the women in this study, impossible. The statement of purpose for immigration detention, where a secure environment is proposed alongside respect for dignity, is simply unmanageable. The use of dignity in this context falls into the trap of the Kantian 'human dignity' in that the term has been used without a real understanding of what dignity feels and looks like for people held in detention.

The natural conclusion then is the abolition of immigration detention. Confinement that has greater legitimacy, such as prison, is known to be painful despite a wealth of protective human rights legislative and the power of legitimacy and justice (Carlton and Segrave, 2011; Hart, 2017; Ryan and Sim, 2016; Moore and Scraton, 2014; Ryan and Ward, 2015; Scott, 2013; Sim, 2009) that are also lacking in immigration removal centres. Similarly, institutions such as the prison still re-enforce unequal power relations in society, especially those surrounding gender and race (Sim, 2009). Immigration detention is an even greater beacon for social inequalities, race particularly, with the majority of people held there noticeably from marginalised groups (Bosworth, 2014). The institution of immigration detention then adds another layer to an already persuasive argument for penal abolitionism (see Gill, 2009; Ryan and Sim, 2016; Ryan and Ward, 2015), particularly when taking into account the questions of legitimacy that remain unanswered when detaining individuals for administrative reasons.

Though dignity as a concept is fraught with criticism and complexity, it clearly meant something to the women in this study, and that makes it an important concept in the context of immigration detention.

In light of this, I would suggest more attention was paid to other sites of care, such as those described in the healthcare literature, such as care homes and hospitals, that have attempted to operationalise dignity for the benefit of individuals within their care. We can learn a lot from institutions that aim to care, rather than punish or expel, individuals. NGOs who promote abolition suggest more holistic approaches to immigration enforcement (IDC, 2015; Ohtani and Phelps, 2016), which, combined with greater focus on the population involved, such as use of the subjective definitions of dignity offered in this work, can go some way to improving the lives of people subject to immigration control in the UK, and after.

Immigration detention fundamentally erodes women's sense of dignity and self-worth. As public concern grows over the treatment of people in detention, and after, particularly the treatment of women (see Canning, 2017), it is timely to review the role of these establishments and their consequences, in order to build an effective critique. Placing matters of dignity at the heart of work on detention offers a new way forward which is grounded in experience, while attentive to the legal framework on which the impact of deprivations to liberty are currently measured. In the introduction to this book, I suggest that the instruments used to measure dignity in detention are based on legal notions of human rights and dignity rather than on the lived experience of people affected by immigration controls, or what is known as 'human dignity' (Habermas, 2010; Misztal, 2012; Shell, 2003). As Bosworth has put it, 'a considerable gap remains between human rights theory and practice in Britain's immigration detention centres' (Bosworth, 2011: 181). I believe the evidence offered in this book supports this theory.

The role of the institution

A common factor across the violations to dignity described by women in this book is that they are caused by the policies and actions directed by the Home Office and the UK government. This is especially important in the discussion of dignity. Negative outcomes after violations to dignity are exacerbated when an individual is exposed to violations over time or when individuals are vulnerable, with the violating actor in a position of power and authority (Chilton, 2006; Jacobson, 2009, 2010; Mann et al., 1994). This is most certainly the case when an individual encounters the immigration estate in the UK, even if detention is not experienced. As detailed earlier, women in the community are still under the control of the Home Office, and thus subject to the power and authority of this institution. However, it appears that if a man or woman is deprived of liberty under immigration powers there are additional aggravating factors that come into play.

When men and women are taken into immigration detention, they are separated from the image of themselves that they have created in their community, and the support mechanisms that maintain this image (Goffman, 1961). This plays out in a varied fashion in immigration removal centres, given the complexity of populations held within them. Without the supportive mechanisms of their former lives, these individuals are particularly vulnerable to the impact of dignity violations. Likewise, women or men who may not have had time to form community bonds and support mechanisms are unable to build them from within removal centres, thus they too are vulnerable. To suffer from a violation of dignity in the community may have the initial emotional reaction of anger, embarrassment, or disbelief; however, the longer-term impact of this violation can be negated by positive reinforcement from other facets of life, such as employment or personal roles such as that of a mother or father. The way in which a person's self can be impacted by their environment can be found in the work of Cohen and Taylor (1972) in their discussion of extreme life experiences and the risk they pose to one's self. They write that in most cases of disturbances to regular life patterns, such as the death of a close family member, the other parts of ourselves provide support for the disturbance. For example, the support of a husband or continued responsibilities to our careers help people to maintain their sense of self-worth. However, in the case of a detained individual, there are few protective roles which can be called on, resulting in an irrevocable shift in how one sees themselves. The sense of self of this population becomes based on how they are treated within that institution. In other words, the dignity-of-self that an individual may have held in the community can become eroded by the dignity-in-relation experienced within a removal centre. This is particularly the case when an individual is removed from their regular life for long periods of time. Some relationships can be maintained for short periods of time, or jobs held open, but over time these relationships and opportunities drift further away (Cohen and Taylor, 1972). In the case of deportation, the act of removing someone from friends, family, and support networks can be permanent. In the case of institutions, it is important to note that violations to dignity 'arise from deliberate decisions, policies, and programs rather than being seen merely as unchangeable life circumstances'

(Chilton, 2006). In the case of removal centres, violations of dignity have arisen from the decisions, policies, and programmes used to implement immigration enforcement. Raising the awareness of dignity violations and the impact of these for individuals allows decision makers to amend policies to reduce the occurrence and impact of violations to dignity in removal centres.

The outsourcing of immigration controls to private companies is also likely to have some bearing on the potential for violations to dignity within removal centres. Of the eight removal centres in the UK, at the time of research, all but one were run by private companies, with the other run by HM prison service.[3] Thus, removal centres are also institutions that are run based on profit motives. It is then possible that greater emphasis is placed on profiteering from expansionism, where more individuals held within these spaces can result in greater profits for the companies involved, than in providing environments that are sympathetic to the needs of the individuals held within removal centres (Bacon, 2005). The outsourcing of removal centre contracts can also result in confusion surrounding the accountability of these institutions to protect the rights of individuals held within them (Bosworth, 2014). It is, thus, not only the institution themselves which can increase the likelihood of violations to dignity for the people held within them, but the overarching policies of the state, which make is easier for responsibilities to be outsourced and possibly avoided.

Can immigration control ever be dignified?

At the outset of this book, I argued that the poor conditions and the negative outcomes of immigration detention apparent in the existing literature suggest there is a disjuncture between dignities, as defined by and protected in legislation, and the experience of those detained in removal centres. My own research firmly supports this split, and I conclude that the current system of immigration enforcement does not fit within a set of liberal human rights norms that we would expect from a country such as the UK. The question that such an observation demands, is why?

According to some border criminologists, matters are simple: the government is deliberately neglecting human rights norms, in order to enforce immigration control. Turnbull (2016) suggests, for example, that making men and women in detention wait is a deliberate tool governments utilise to emphasise their power. Removing people from the community effectively 'others' such people and furthers the government's attempts to remove them from the country (Grewlock, 2015). Removing women from the community, in both this project and in other works (Bosworth and Turnbull, 2015a; Canning, 2017; Hasselberg, 2016), severs the links they held in the community. The longer men and women are detained, the greater the effect of their 'othering,' and with it, the erosion of their ability to fight removal with the help of personal networks and local legal and community support (Canning, 2017).

For women released from detention, the displacement and restriction of access to work, education, and social interaction prevented them from participating as full members of the UK community (Canning, 2017). Like detention, this more subtle form of exclusion facilitates their removal as it creates a group of people who are considered undesirable and thus disposable (Grewlock, 2015; Turnbull, 2017). These arguments are supported by Bosworth and Turnbull in their discussion on penal power and immigration detention who point out how the marking of people in detention as the other who do not belong in the UK aids in the objectification of this population, and ultimately allows them to be dehumanised and expelled (Bosworth and Turnbull, 2015b).

The temporal uncertainties of detention, which can be simultaneously suspended and frenzied, renders those subjects unable to wield agency. Women and men in detention find it difficult to plan for any outcome (Griffiths, 2013, 2014). This, for Griffiths, is a tool of power that is inherent in an incoherent and impenetrable immigration system, which further helps in the government's aims to remove people from the country. Gill (2009b) adds to this argument in his analysis of the forced mobility of men around the detention estate as an example of governmental power. He suggests the seemingly unnecessary movement of men between removal centres reaffirms them as transitory and depersonalised. Such strategies make it harder for people to obtain help to fight their detention and removal, and thus makes it easier to deport them (Gill, 2009b, 2009a).

Canning (2017) argues that the asylum system of the UK is a form of structural violence. The harms caused to women by the government are not only avoidable, she points out, but also foreseeable and foreseen by those in power. Canning's argument is well supported by a body of literature that presents evidence for the way in which the government control and deter people seeking asylum by means of policies which cause poverty and deprivation (Allsopp et al., 2014; Bloch and

Schuster, 2002, 2005a), displacement (Bloch and Schuster, 2005b), and the securitisation of borders (Wilson, 2015). Considering this evidence, and that of this book, it is difficult to argue that the harms caused to women in detention and after are not intentional. However, there does exist another layer to the problem of dignity violations that suggests human rights norms are not so much ignored as misinterpreted due to their ambiguity.

There are many criticisms of legal frameworks surrounding human rights protections. In the opening chapters of this book, I explored a small section of literature pertaining to the concept of dignity. There I explained how I focused this project on phenomenological approaches to dignity, which conceive the concept as a socially constructed matter. Legal frameworks, conversely, rely on the more metaphysical definition of human dignity, that it is something all humans are bestowed with, and that it must be protected, with little regard to the conceptualisation of the notion (Dales, 1977; Guerra, 2001; Johnson, 1971; Korsgaard, 1992; Sensen, 2009). As may then be expected, the criticisms of dignity in legal frameworks often centre around the ambiguity and vagueness of the concept (Birnbacher, 1996; Hailer and Ritschl, 1996; Jacobson, 2009). This is perhaps the cause of the disjuncture between the apparent attempts of the UK government's Home Office to secure dignified treatment in detention and after, and the lived reality presented by the women in this study.

Human rights frameworks have, however, been used to successfully challenge some aspects of immigration detention (Canning, 2017). As an example, when I began this research in 2015, pregnant women were held in immigration detention indefinitely. At the time of writing, they are now subject to release 72 hours after the Home Office confirms they are pregnant. This development was enshrined in the 2016 Immigration Act, after lobbying by lawyers and NGOs using various human rights legislation to support their case (see, for example, Girma et al., 2015; Medical Justice, 2013). This evidence provides support for the former argument that the government have in fact neglected human rights norms, and while promising in its incitement of change, the effective challenge of detention practices is time consuming, expensive, and a great deal more effort would be required to ensure all damaging aspects of detention are remedied (Canning, 2017).

Despite the ambiguity and complexity of human rights norms there are, however, institutions in the UK in which human rights norms have resulted in substantially improved treatment of the populations which require their protection. The health and social care literature referred to in the opening chapters of this book provides numerous examples of the ways in which human rights norms can be conceptualised into effective frameworks. For example, ensuring patients in hospital have privacy has been shown to ensure their sense of dignity (Aranda et al., 2010; Gennip et al., 2013; Hemati et al., 2016). Another case, provided by Hemati et al. in their conceptualisation of dignity in end-of-life care, illustrated how respecting privacy was conceptualised by closing hospital curtains and ensuring other patients could not overhear sensitive conversations regarding their treatment (Hemati et al., 2016). Other works in healthcare also recognise the importance of respecting the different cultural and religious norms surrounding privacy in their treatment (Loggers et al., 2013; Sautier et al., 2014; Scarre, 2012). Using the definitions and desire for privacy provided by women in this book, similar conceptualisations could be developed for those involved in immigration enforcement processes. Women who were victims of trafficking or sexual and gendered violence, for example, should be provided with greater levels of privacy in respect for their experience; for example, if a woman desires so, the use of female-only housing in the community.

Exceptions to the rule of harm

In the opening paragraph of this section, I presented my conclusion that the current system of immigration enforcement does not fit within a set of liberal human rights norms that we would expect from a country such as the UK. However, in this book one important exception to the overarching findings of offence and harm to women was found and is deserving of analysis. Half the women I spoke to in Jamaica had never spent free time in the British community. They had been incarcerated in prisons and had then passed through immigration detention on their way back to Jamaica. This very specific group of women did not appear to suffer the indignities of their counterparts. Rather, they saw detention as part of their transition to going home and, importantly, going home is what they wanted. The only problem they had with detention was the fact that it delayed their going home by a day or two.

The experiences of these women pose a difficult question for abolitionists of immigration detention, as it suggests that if used in a very particular way, immigration detention poses no harm to some women.

Given the small sample of women and that this finding was retrospective during analysis, it is difficult to ascertain exactly why this was the case. Yet, there are certain characteristics of their experience which may explain the lack of harm caused. The first, is that these women never expected to stay in the UK. They had all committed a crime, were given a corresponding sentence, and knew that on completion of that sentence they would return to Jamaica. Thus, their departure from the country was considered just. Though some women did not realise the consequences of their actions at the time of the offence, they also accepted that the punishment handed to them was fair. The second is that this group of women had never spent time in the UK community. Therefore, they were not subject to the 'othering' experienced by many women by their detention, nor did they spend time in limbo living under Home Office regulations in the community. As a result, this group also avoided the offences to autonomy, diminishment, and vilification that detention and immigration control caused to the other women in this study. Importantly, it is also not the case that these women were somehow immune to dignity violations as they did then suffer the criminalisation, labelling, and stigma common to all people deported to Jamaica.

This finding is particularly interesting, because it suggests that if immigration removal centres were used as short term, transient spaces, in the way in which they were initially intended to be, they may not be the damaging spaces they are now typically found to be. Perhaps this is the cause of the disjuncture between rights and experience, where the government and Home Office policies have not caught up with the changing usage of removal centres. But nevertheless, following the arguments of the scholars here, and that of my own work, the policy and practical implications for immigration enforcement as they stand are that these systems do not adequately care for the dignity of the women that they are duty bound to protect. At the very least, these findings support the current groundswell of calls for a time limit in the UK detention system voiced from NGOs, charities, and official bodies such as the All-Party Parliamentary Group on Refugees, the All-Party Parliamentary Group on Migration (APPG on Refugees and APPG on Migration, 2015), and the *Review into the Welfare in Detention of Vulnerable Persons* from Shaw (2016).

Alternatives to detention

In light of my findings, and those of others, regarding the damaging impact of incarceration for immigration purposes (especially Bosworth,

2014; Canning, 2017; Coffey et al., 2010; Hasselberg, 2016; Kellezi and Bosworth, 2016; McLoughlin and Warin, 2008; Shaw, 2016; Silove et al., 2001; Steel and Silove, 2001), the argument for abolition of immigration detention in its current form is easy to make. There exists a substantial breadth of literature which argues any confinement is structured to be painful, even those institutions which are somewhat less contested, such as the prison (Carlton and Segrave, 2011; Hart, 2017; Moore and Scraton, 2014; Ryan and Sim, 2016; Ryan and Ward, 2015; Scott, 2013; Sim, 2009). In Sim's work on prisons, power, and the state, he highlights the role of the prison in re-enforcing unequal power relations within society, such as those of gender and race. Similarly, he argues that sustained criticisms and reform has failed to mend the damages caused by incarceration and that an abolitionist position is thusly a better alternative (Ryan and Sim, 2016; Sim, 2009). On women, the call for alternatives to prison increase, with evidence of pains suffered by this group beyond those intentioned for and incurred by men by design (Carlton and Segrave, 2011; Moore and Scraton, 2014). Immigration detention similarly re-enforces social inequalities, as those held within removal centres are also predominantly from marginalised social groups (Bosworth, 2014). Likewise, the increasing penal powers of the state in relation to immigration detention reflect those of the prison (Bosworth et al., 2016; Bosworth, 2017; Bosworth and Turnbull, 2015a), which are already criticised heavily in prison abolitionist literature (Gill, 2009b; Ryan and Sim, 2016; Ryan and Ward, 2015), without the additional questions regarding the moral decision to detain individuals for administrative purposes.

But what are the alternatives? The findings in this book from women held in the community, and those in studies which focus on the lives of people seeking asylum in the UK community (Allsopp et al., 2014; Bloch and Schuster, 2005; Canning, 2017; Klein and Williams, 2012) illustrate that, even without detention, people under immigration control in the community are already treated in a way that is damaging to their dignity. It is thus not as simple as suggesting current community-based practices are the answer. There has been a shift away from immigration detention practices by the UK government, with increased pressure and criticism regarding the economic and personal cost of the practice (Ohtani and Phelps, 2016). The review conducted by Stephen Shaw, who was also responsible for the review into vulnerable adults in detention published in 2016 (Shaw, 2016), was conclusive in its call for a need to change the way immigration detention functioned, and some good has come from this work, such as greater freedom of movement within removal centres. But it is not enough.

Alternatives proposed by Detention Action (Ohtani and Phelps, 2016) and the International Detention Coalition (IDC) (IDC, 2015) are based on a holistic approach to immigration enforcement. They work on a presumption against detention and on minimum standards in the community which encompass: Respect for fundamental rights, basic needs, formal status and documentation, legal advice and interpretation, fair and timely case resolution, and regular review of placement decisions. In light of the conclusions of this book, there is promise to these findings; however, it would be wise to be wary of the reliance on legal rights frameworks for the reasons outlined above.

Nonetheless, the research conducted for this book could go some way to assist in the development of the humane immigration enforcement practices suggested by Detention Action and the IDC. As suggested earlier, the conceptual frameworks developed by health and social care practitioners in relation to dignity in care have illustrated the use of practical examinations of the concept of dignity such as the one offered in my own work. The introduction of the right to work, for example, provides a practical example which could reduce the dependence of individuals on the government and promote self-worth and self-esteem. In combination with the holistic approaches outlined by Detention Action and the IDC in their reports (Ohtani and Phelps, 2016; IDC, 2015), perhaps there is hope for improved conditions for the population subject to immigration control in the UK.

Conclusion

States like the UK remain committed to immigration enforcement practices, notwithstanding their damaging effects. As I argue in this book, legal protections based in human rights frameworks, however important, are insufficient to protect those held within removal centres. Likewise, women in the community appear subject to a regime that shows little respect for the dignity of those under immigration control and women removed to Jamaica provide a case study of difficult conditions that are at least partially the consequence of their treatment by the UK government. If the UK is to fully commit to its obligations to protect vulnerable populations under international law and moral duty, then it is clear that something needs to change, dramatically.

Acknowledgement

Gerlach, A. (2022) 'Women's experiences of indignity in immigration detention and beyond', Incarceration. doi: 10.1177/26326663221103437. Parts of this work have been reproduced in this chapter with permission of SAGE Publications.

Notes

1 The name of Maria's community has been hidden to maintain anonymity.
2 Notably, these are all symptoms commonly ascribed to people suffering from severe stress.
3 This centre, IRC Morton Hall, has since closed.

References

APPG on Refugees and APPG on Migration (2015) *The Report of the Inquiry into the Use of Immigration Detention in the United Kingdom*. London: House of Commons.

Allsopp J, Sigona N and Phillimore J (2014) *Poverty among Refugees and Asylum Seekers in the UK an Evidence and Policy Review*. IRiS Working Paper Series: 1–46.

Aranda K, Jones A, Sussex E and Projects H (2010) Dignity in health-care: A critical exploration using feminism and theories of recognition. *Nursing Inquiry* 17(3): 248–256.

Bacon C (2005) The evolution of immigration detention in the UK: The involvement of private prison companies. In: *Refugee Studies Centre Working Papers* (Issue 27). University of Oxford, Refugee Studies Centre, p. 146. https://doi.org/10.1111/j.1467-629X.1980.tb00220.x.

BID (2009) Out of sight, out of mind: Experiences of immigration detention in the UK what is bail for immigration detainees? http://www.biduk.org/download.php?id=6.

Birnbacher D (1996) Ambiguities in the concept of Menschenwurde. In: Bayertz K (ed.) *Sanctity of Life and Human Dignity*. New York: Kluwer Academic Publishers, pp. 107–121.

Bloch A and Schuster L (2002) Asylum and welfare: Contemporary debates. *Critical Social Policy* 22(3): 393–414.

Bloch A and Schuster L (2005a) Asylum policy under new labour. *City Research Online Original* 13(132): 115–118. https://doi.org/10.1016/j.cpr.2010.02.004.

Bloch A and Schuster L (2005b) At the extremes of exclusion: Deportation, detention and dispersal. *Ethnic and Racial Studies* 28(3): 491–512. https://doi.org/10.1080/0141987042000337858.

Bosworth M (2011) Human rights and immigration detention in the United Kingdom. In: Dembour M-B and Kelly T (eds.) *Are Human Rights for*

Migrants? Critical Reflections on the Status of Irregular Migrants in Europe and the United States. London: Routledge, pp. 165–183.
Bosworth M (2014) *Inside Immigration Detention*. Oxford: Oxford University Press.
Bosworth M (2017) Immigration detention and penal power: A criminological perspective. In: Flynn MJ and Flynn MB (eds.) *Challenging Immigration Detention—Academics, Activists, Policymakers*. Cheltenham: Edward Elgar, pp. 52–65.
Bosworth M, Hasselberg I and Turnbull S (2016a) Imprisonment in a global age: Rethinking penal power. In: Jewkes Y, Crewe B and Bennett J (eds.) *Handbook of Prisons*. 2nd ed. London: Routledge.
Bosworth M, Hasselberg I and Turnbull S (2016b) Punishment, citizenship and identity: An Introduction. *Criminology and Criminal Justice* 16(3): 257–266. https://doi.org/10.1177/1748895816635720.
Bosworth M and Turnbull S (2015a) Immigration detention, punishment and the criminalization of migration. In: Pickering S and Ham J (eds.) *The Routledge Handbook on Crime and International Migration*. 1st ed. Routledge, pp. 91–106.
Bosworth M and Turnbull S (2015b) Immigration detention and the expansion of penal power in the UK. In: Reiter K and Koenig A (eds.) *Extreme Punishment*. London: Palgrave, pp. 50–67.
Canning V (2017) *Gendered Harm and Structural Violence in the British Asylum System*. Routledge. https://doi.org/10.4324/9781315720975.
Carlton B and Segrave M (2011) Women's survival post-imprisonment: Connecting imprisonment with pains past and present. *Punishment and Society* 13(5): 551–570. https://doi.org/10.1177/1462474511422174.
Chilton M (2006) Developing a measure of dignity for stress-related health outcomes. *Health and Human Rights* 9(2): 208–233. https://doi.org/10.2307/4065408.
Coffey GJ, Kaplan I, Sampson RC and Tucci MM (2010) The meaning and mental health consequences of long-term immigration detention for people seeking asylum. *Social Science and Medicine* 70(12): 2070–2079. https://doi.org/10.1016/j.socscimed.2010.02.042.
Cohen S and Taylor L (1972) *Psychological Survival: The Experience of Long-Term Imprisonment*. London: Penguin Books Ltd.
Dales RC (1977) A medieval view of human dignity. *Journal of the History of Ideals* 38(4): 557–572. http://ojs.libraries.psu.edu/index.php/phj/article/viewFile/21299/21068.
Dupré C (2009) Unlocking human dignity: Towards a theory for the 21st century. *European Human Rights Law Review* 2: 190–205.
Gallagher A and Seedhouse D (2002) Dignity in care: The views of patients and relatives. *Nursing Times* 98(43): 38–41.
Gennip IE Van, Pasman HRW, Oosterveld-Vlug MG, Willems DL and Onwuteaka-Philipsen BD (2013) The development of a model of dignity in illness based on qualitative interviews with seriously ill patients. *International*

Journal of Nursing Studies 50(8): 1080–1089. https://doi.org/10.1016/j.ijnurstu.2012.12.014.

Gill N (2009a) Governmental mobility: The power effects of the movement of detained asylum seekers around Britain's detention estate. *Political Geography* 28(3): 186–196. https://doi.org/10.1016/j.polgeo.2009.05.003.

Gill N (2009b) Presentational state power: Temporal and spatial influences over asylum sector decisionmakers. *Transactions of the Institute of British Geographers* 34(2): 215–233. https://doi.org/10.1111/j.1475-5661.2009.00337.x.

Girma M, Kershaw I, Lousley G, Radice S and Walter N (2015) *I am Human: Refugee Women's Experiences of Detention in the UK*. London: Women for Refugee Women, pp. 1–32.

Goffman I (1961) *Asylums: Essays on the Social Situation of Mental Patients and Other Inmates*. New York: Anchor Books.

Grewlock M (2015) Reinventing 'the stain': Bad character and criminal deportation in contemporary Australia. In: Pickering S and Ham J (eds.) *The Routledge Handbook on Crime and International Migration*. London: Routledge.

Griffiths M (2013) Living with uncertainty: Indefinite immigration detention. *Journal of Legal Anthropology* 1(3): 263–286. https://doi.org/10.4059/jla.2013.2616.

Griffiths M (2014) Out of time: The temporal uncertainties of refused asylum seekers and immigration detainees. *Journal of Ethnic and Migration Studies* 40(12): 1991–2009. https://doi.org/10.1080/1369183X.2014.907737.

Guerra MD (2001) The affirmation of genuine human dignity. *The Journal of Markets and Morality* 4(2): 295–301.

Habermas J (2010) The concept of human dignity and the realistic Utopia of human rights. *Metaphilosophy* 41(4): 464–480. https://doi.org/10.1111/j.1467-9973.2010.01648.x.

Hailer M and Ritschl D (1996) The general notion of human dignity and the specific arguments in medical ethics. In Bayertz K (ed.) *Sanctity of Life and Human Dignity*. Dordrecht: Kluwer Academic Publishers, pp. 91–106.

Halliday TC and Liu S (2021) Dignity discourses in struggles for basic legal freedoms in China. *Asian Journal of Law and Society* 8(1): 134–150. https://doi.org/10.1017/als.2020.40.

Hart EL (2017) Women prisoners and the drive for desistance: Capital and responsibilization as a barrier to change. *Women and Criminal Justice* 27(3): 151–169. https://doi.org/10.1080/08974454.2016.1217814.

Hasselberg I (2016) *Enduring Uncertainty: Deportation, Punishment and Everyday Life*. Oxford: Berghahn.

Hemati Z, Ashouri E, Allahbakhshian M, Pourfarzad Z, Shirani F, Safazadeh S, Ziyaei M, Varzeshnejad M, Hashemi M and Taleghani F (2016) Dying with dignity: A concept analysis. *Journal of Clinical Nursing* 25(9–10): 1218–1228. https://doi.org/10.1111/jocn.13143.

Henry LM, Rushton C, Beach MC and Faden R (2015) Respect and dignity: A conceptual model for patients in the intensive care unit. *Narrative Inquiry in Bioethics* 5(1A): 5A–14A.

HM Inspectorate of Prisons, & Independent Chief Inspector of Borders and Immigration (2012) *The Effectiveness and Impact of Immigration Detention Casework: A Joint Thematic Review by HM Inspectorate of Prisons and the Independent Chief Inspector of Borders and Immigration December 2012 (Issue December).*

IDC (2015) There are alternatives. International Detention Coalition. http://idcoalition.org/wp-content/uploads/dlm_uploads/2015/10/idcTAA.pdf.

Jacobson N (2009) A taxonomy of dignity: A grounded theory study. *BMC International Health and Human Rights* 9: 3. https://doi.org/10.1186/1472-698X-9-3.

Jacobson N (2010) *Dignity and Health*. Nashville: Vanderbilt University Press.

Johnson JP (1971) Human dignity and the nature of society. *World Futures* 10(3): 213–248. https://doi.org/10.1080/02604027.1971.9971751.

Kellezi B and Bosworth M (2016) *Mental Health, Suicidal Thoughts and Self-Harm inside Immigration Detention (Issue November).* Oxford: Oxford University.

Klein A and Williams L (2012) Immigration detention in the community: Research on the experiences of migrants released from detention centres in the UK. *Population, Space and Place* 18(6): 741–753. https://doi.org/10.1002/psp.1725.

Korsgaard C (1992) Creating the kingdom of ends: Reciprocity and responsibility in personal relations. *Philosphical Perspectives* 6: 305–332. https://doi.org/10.2307/2214250.

Loggers ET, Starks H, Shannon-Dudley M, Back AL, Appelbaum FR and Stewart FM (2013) Implementing a death with dignity program at a comprehensive cancer center. *New England Journal of Medicine* 368(15): 1417–1424. https://doi.org/10.1056/NEJMsa1213398.

Malcolm J (2016). The colonial representation of Jihadi John: Matters of life and death in the "war on terror". *Soundings* 62: 138–149.

Mann J, Gostin L, Gruskin S, Brennan T, Lazzarini Z and Fineberg HV (1994) Health and human rights. *Health and Human Rights* 1(1): 6–23. https://doi.org/10.2307/4065260.

McLoughlin P and Warin M (2008) Corrosive places, inhuman spaces: Mental health in Australian immigration detention. *Health and Place* 14(2): 254–264. https://doi.org/10.1016/j.healthplace.2007.06.008.

Medical Justice (2013) *Expecting Change: The Case for Ending the Detention of Pregnant Women*. Medical Justice, pp. 1–86. London: Medical Justice.

Misztal BA (2012) The idea of dignity: Its modern significance. *European Journal of Social Theory* 16(1): 101–121. https://doi.org/10.1177/1368431012449237.

Moore L and Scraton P (2014) *The Incarceration of Women: Punishing Bodies, Breaking Spirits*. London: Palgrave Macmillan.

Nussbaum MC (1947–1997) Capabilities and human rights. *Fordham Law Review* 66: 273–300.

Ohtani E and Phelps J (2016) *Without Detention*. Opportunities for Alternatives. London: Detention Action.

Phelps J (2009) *Detained Lives: The Real Cost of Indefinite Immigration Detention*. (January). London: Detention Action.

Ryan M and Sim J (2016) Campaigning for and campaigning against prisons: Excavating and reaffirming the case for prison abolition. In: Jewkes R, Crewe B and Bennet J (eds.) *Handbook on Prisons*. 2nd ed. London: Routledge.

Ryan M and Ward T (2015) Prison abolition in the UK: They dare not speak its name? *Social Justice* 41(3): 107–119. http://search.ebscohost.com/login.aspx?direct=true&db=i3h&AN=102017441&site=ehost-live.

Sautier LP, Vehling S and Mehnert A (2014) Assessment of patients' dignity in cancer care: Preliminary psychometrics of the German version of the patient dignity inventory (PDI-G). *Journal of Pain and Symptom Management* 47(1): 181–188. https://doi.org/10.1016/j.jpainsymman.2013.02.023.

Scarre G (2012) Can there be a good death? *Journal of Evaluation in Clinical Practice* 18(5): 1082–1086. https://doi.org/10.1111/j.1365-2753.2012.01922.x.

Scott D (2013) The politics of prisoner legal rights. *Howard Journal of Criminal Justice* 52(3): 233–250. https://doi.org/10.1111/hojo.12017.

Sensen O (2009) Kant's conception of human dignity. *Kant-Studien* 100(3): 309–331. https://doi.org/10.1515/KANT.2009.018.

Shaw S (2016) *Review into the Welfare in Detention of Vulnerable Persons: A Report to the Home Office by Stephen Shaw*. London: HMSO, CM9186.

Shell SM (2003) Kant on human dignity. In: Kraynak MP and Tinder EG (eds.) *In Defence of Human Dignity: Essays for Our Times*. Indiana: University of Notre Dame Press, pp. 53–80.

Silove D, Steel Z and Mollica RF (2001) Detention of asylum seekers: Assault on health, human rights, and social development. *The Lancet* 357(9266): 1436–1437. https://doi.org/10.1016/S0140-6736(00)04575-X.

Sim J (2009) *Punishment and Prisons: Power and the Carceral State*. London: SAGE Publications, Ltd.

Steel Z and Silove DM (2001) The mental health implications of detaining asylum seekers. *The Medical Journal of Australia* 175(11–12): 596–599.

Stoecker R (2011) Three crucial turns on the road to an adequate understanding of human dignity. In: Kaufmann P, Kuch H, Neuhauser C and Webster E (eds.) *Humiliation, Degradation, Dehumanization: Human Dignity Violated*. New York: Springer, pp. 7–17.

Sugarman J, Branyon E, Carrese J, Faden R, Forbes L, Geller G, Kass N and Henry LM (2015) Toward treatment with respect and dignity in the intensive care unit. *Narrative Inquiry in Bioethics* 5(1A): 1A–4A.

Turnbull S (2016) "Stuck in the middle": Waiting and uncertainty in immigration detention. *Time and Society* 25(1): 61–79. https://doi.org/10.1177/0961463X15604518.

Turnbull S (2017) Starting again: Life after deportation from the UK. In: Khosravi S (ed.) *After Deportation: Ethnographic Perspectives*. London: Palgrave Macmillan, pp. 37–62.

Wilson D (2015) Border militarisation, technology and crime control. In: Pickering S and Ham J (eds.) *The Routledge Handbook of Crime and Migration Studies*. London: Routledge.

INDEX

For Product Safety Concerns and Information please contact our EU representative GPSR@taylorandfrancis.com
Taylor & Francis Verlag GmbH, Kaufingerstraße 24, 80331 München, Germany

www.ingramcontent.com/pod-product-compliance
Ingram Content Group UK Ltd.
Pitfield, Milton Keynes, MK11 3LW, UK
UKHW022311250926
475702UK00046B/679
* 9 7 8 0 3 6 7 4 2 2 8 0 6 *